GREAT NAVAL DISASTERS

Kit & Carolyn Bonner

MBI Publishing Company

First published in 1998 by MBI Publishing Company, 729 Prospect Avenue, PO Box 1, Osceola, WI 54020-0001 USA

MBI Publishing Company books are also available at discounts in bulk quantity for industrial or sales-promotional use. For details write to Special Sales Manager at Motorbooks International Wholesalers & Distributors, 729 Prospect Avenue, Osceola, WI 54020-0001 USA.

Library of Congress Cataloging-in-Publication Data
Bonner, Kermit.
Great naval disasters: U.S. naval accidents in the 20th century/Kermit "Kit" Bonner & Carolyn Bonner.
    p. cm.
    Includes index.
    ISBN 0-7603-0594-3 (pbk.: alk. paper)
    1. United States. Navy—History—20th century. 2. Marine accidents—United Staes. I. Bonner, Carolyn. II. Title.
VA58.4.B66   1998
363.12'32'0973—dc21   98-36675

Photos credited to TIM - SFCB are from the Treasure Island Museum-San Francisco Call Bulletin, TIM is just the Treasure Island Museum, SFMM is the San Francisco Maritime Museum, and USNI is the United States Naval Institute. Their contributions to this work are greatly appreciated.

On the front cover: The U.S.S. *S P Lee* DD-310 makes smoke on a speed run shortly before she and her squadron ran aground on the night of September 8, 1923. This bizarre incident took the lives of 23 seamen and caused the total loss of seven modern U.S. Navy destroyers valued at $13.5 million. *Author's Collection*

On the back cover, top: The U.S.S. *S P Lee* DD-310 is in the foreground, and the hull has obviously buckled just forward of the starboard torpedo mount. The U.S.S. *Nicholas* DD-311 has broken in two in the background. *Author's Collection*

On the back cover, bottom: The bow and upper forward deck of the *Mary Luckenbach* show the results of her collision with the U.S. Navy hospital ship U.S.S. *Benevolence* AH-13. While the damage to the *Mary Luckenbach* was substantial, she faired much better than the *Benevolence*, which foundered and sank in shoal water. No one aboard the freighter was killed or injured in the collision. *SFMM*

Printed in the United States of America

CONTENTS

PREFACE

In the century since the Spanish-American War, the United States has dedicated much of its treasure and effort to having a navy "second to none." By 1945, the goal had been realized and at the turn of the twenty-first century, the U.S. Navy is still the largest and most capable sea force in the world. The number of ships has shrunk (comparative to World War II and the Cold War), yet technological capability has taken a quantum leap. Virtually all aspects of naval warfare are now subject to mechanization and computerization. But without the men and women of the naval service, a navy is merely a collection of microchips encased in steel hulls. A navy relies on dedicated men and women who go to the sea in ships, and—despite automation—it will always be the crew that ultimately defends and protects its ship.

This book is dedicated to the men and women who serve and have served in the U.S. Navy. It is an honorable but dangerous profession; at any time disaster can strike. The Navy has successfully reduced the incidence of tragedy through new techniques and by stressing constant vigilance. Yet despite the best and thoroughly tested safety systems, accidents resulting in death, injury, and the loss of Navy property can happen. *Great Naval Disasters: U.S. Navy Accidents in the Twentieth Century* graphically demonstrates what can happen during a crisis aboard a warship and how innocent mistakes can cause great loss of life.

This book is also dedicated to the 1,310 people who perished on the ships featured, the scores of injured, and the rescuers who courageously saved so many at the risk of their own lives.

A warship is a complicated and diverse system often requiring hundreds and sometimes thousands of personnel to successfully operate it. Most carry tons of munitions in the form of rockets, guided missiles, torpedoes, mines, projectiles, powder bags, and bombs. Many warships also must carry several tons of flammable fuel and in some cases a nuclear power plant for propulsion. Warships are dangerous and accident prone due to the fact that they travel on an uncontrolled and unpredictable sea and must be ready at any time to engage an enemy.

The primary noncombat threats to a warship are collision, grounding, explosion, fire, and the age-old curse of foundering. Since the beginning of the twentieth century, the U.S. Navy has experienced 75 major accidents that have resulted in the loss of life and substantial damage to its vessels. Added to this are hundreds of minor accidents, many of which are just plain embarrassing, but all costing taxpayer dollars.

Significant U.S. Navy accidents in the twentieth century began with the loss of 60 men on July 21, 1905. A boiler exploded on the gunboat U.S.S. *Bennington* PG-4, when she was moored in San Diego, California. Ironically, the next ship christened U.S.S. *Bennington* was an *Essex*-class carrier that lost 103 men when an explosion and fire wracked her nearly a half century later.

Major fires have consumed many ships, including the destroyer tender U.S.S. *Prairie* AD-15 in September 1942 and the aircraft carrier U.S.S. *Leyte* CV-32 in October 1953. The fires aboard the *Leyte* killed 37 men and injured 28 others.

No less deadly have been the accidents involving submarines. By its very nature, submarine duty is more hazardous than almost any in the Navy.

Since the turn of the century, the Navy has lost at least 15 boats due to noncombat reasons. The first major loss was the submarine *F-4*, which was lost off Pearl Harbor on February 25, 1915, with the loss of 22 men. The latest casualty was the *Guitarro* SSN-665, which sank dockside at the Mare Island Naval Shipyard on May 15, 1969. There was no loss of life, but much explanation was necessary.

The most common accidents center on collision and grounding.

Collisions at sea often result in the loss of lives and vessels. On April 26, 1952, the U.S.S. *Wasp* CV-18 ran over the U.S.S. *Hobson* DMS-26 during night flight operations—176 men, including the

The U.S.S. *Prairie* AD-15 burns dockside in Newfoundland. The gunboat U.S.S. *Spry* PG-64, moored behind the destroyer tender, caught fire and it spread to the *Prairie*. No lives were lost, but the tender suffered extensive damage. *TIM - SFCB*

5

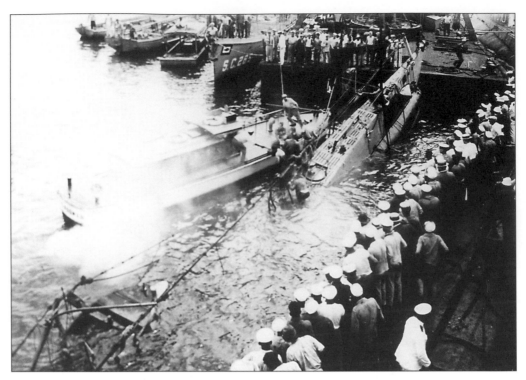

The submarine *S-4* is recovered after sinking on December 19, 1927. The U.S.C.G. *Cutter Paulding* had rammed her; 40 lives were lost. *TIM - SFCB*

captain, lost their lives. Four years later, the battleship U.S.S. *Wisconsin* BB-64 collided with the destroyer U.S.S. *Eaton* DDE-510 in the fog. Fortunately, no lives were lost.

Groundings rarely cause death or injury and are the most common of all accidents. The grounding of the battleship U.S.S. *Missouri* BB-63 was certainly spectacular; however, she was not the only U.S. capital ship to run aground in the twentieth century. Even sister ship U.S.S. *Wisconsin* BB-64 ran aground in the Hudson River on August 22, 1951. She was freed by 11 tugs two hours later. Earlier in the century (June 1924), the new battleship U.S.S. *West Virginia* BB-48 slid up on the mud in Hampton Roads and remained until pulled loose six hours later. Her captain had just been selected for flag rank,

and was publicly humiliated. Sister ship U.S.S. *Colorado* BB-45 grounded in New York Harbor in May 1927, and the U.S.S. *Tennessee* BB-43 nearly became a permanent part of San Francisco Bay in the early 1930s. Aircraft carriers were not immune as demonstrated by the short-lived grounding of the U.S.S. *Saratoga* CV-3 off Long Beach, California, on August 18, 1932; and fifty years later the U.S.S. *Enterprise* CVAN-65 touched bottom in San Francisco Bay.

Great Naval Disasters: U.S. Navy Accidents in the Twentieth Century chronicles the tragedies that have befallen 19 U.S. Navy warships since 1900. Some resulted from foolhardiness, others from carelessness, and still others from an arrogant disrespect for the sea and ships. All, however, ended in the same fashion—sadly.

The damaged bow of the battleship U.S.S. *Wisconsin* BB-64 after colliding with the destroyer U.S.S. *Eaton* DDE-510 in a heavy fog on May 6, 1956. The problem was solved quickly by removing a 68-foot bow section of the unfinished sister ship *Kentucky* and attaching it to the *Wisconsin*. The *Kentucky* was later scrapped. *TIM - SFCB*

While being towed to the Philadelphia Navy Yard from New York, the *Fletcher*-class destroyer U.S.S. *Monssen* DD-798 broke loose and was later found on the beach in New Jersey. No lives were lost. *TIM - SFCB*

In a rare photograph, the U.S. Navy's third aircraft carrier, U.S.S. *Saratoga* CV-3, rests on a sandy bottom just south of Long Beach, California. She was freed a few hours later. *TIM - SFCB*

The battleship U.S.S. *Colorado* BB-45 sits on the rocks off Governors Island on May 5, 1927. After off-loading much of her stores and munitions, she was refloated. *TIM - SFCB*

The U.S.S. *Wisconsin* is pulled and pushed off the mud in the Hudson River in late August 1951. She was stuck a mere two hours. *TIM - SFCB*

CHAPTER ONE

COLLISION AND GROUNDING

U.S. Navy Hospital Ship *Benevolence* AH-13
Lost Outside the Golden Gate

On August 25, 1950, the freighter *Mary Luckenbach* rammed and sunk the modern U.S. Navy Hospital Ship *Benevolence* AH-13 in the main ship channel just outside the entrance to San Francisco Bay. Both ships were equipped with radar and their captains were aware of the dangers inherent in the ship channel leading into the San Francisco harbor. On that afternoon, the danger was increased by thick fog. The *Benevolence* was rammed at least twice and quickly foundered in shoal water. Of the 526 men and women aboard, miraculously, all but 18 survived during a rescue effort that took many hours. Many of the survivors were injured and suffered the effects of exposure.

Hospital Ship Benevolence *AH-3*

The *Benevolence* did not begin her career as a fleet hospital ship, but as an assembly line C-4 cargo freighter with the intended name of *Marine Lion*. She was built pursuant to a Maritime Administration contract by the Sun Shipbuilding Company in Chester, Pennsylvania. On July

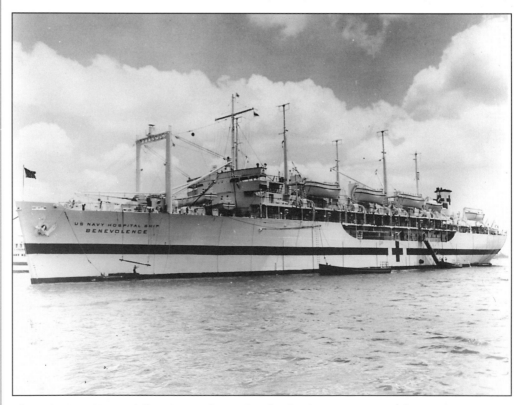

The U.S. Navy Hospital Ship *Benevolence* shortly after being converted from a C-4 freighter hull in 1945. *USNI*

Hospital ship *Benevolence* AH-13 at sea at the end of World War II. This ship participated in "Operation Crossroads," a nuclear bomb testing at Bikini Atoll. *USNI*

10, 1944, the *Marine Lion* was launched; but before being fitted out, the Navy instructed that she be converted to a hospital ship. Casualties in the Pacific War were mounting, and additional hospital ships were needed. On May 12, 1945, she was commissioned as the *Benevolence* and went to sea.

The *Benevolence* displaced 15,400 tons full load and was 529 feet in length with a 71.5-foot beam. She was powered by steam turbines and could make up to 18.3 knots turning a single shaft. The crew capacity of the *Benevolence* was 570 including medical personnel. She was a fully functioning, all-purpose medical facility and could accommodate 800 patients. Overall there were six C-4 freighters converted to hospital ships as the war progressed.

The *Benevolence* entered the Pacific War zone in late July 1945 and immediately began to care for the wounded emerging from fleet operations off Okinawa. There would be great

need for hospital ships with the planned invasion of the Japanese homeland, but the nuclear weapons detonated over Hiroshima and Nagasaki prompted the Japanese government to sue for peace.

After the war ended, the *Benevolence* crew treated allied prisoners of war and transported the wounded back to the United States. The hospital ship made three round-trips from Pearl Harbor to San Francisco carrying wounded. The Navy chose to scrap or lay up in mothballs many ships, yet the Navy selected the *Benevolence* for two more assignments prior to retirement. In April 1946, she was attached to Joint Task Force 1 for station duty to receive and treat any casualties from the July 1946 nuclear tests at Bikini Atoll in the Marshall Islands. After "Operation Crossroads" was complete, she was detached and sent to China to treat patients in the Tsingtao area. This completed, she returned to San Francisco and was placed in reserve on September 13, 1947.

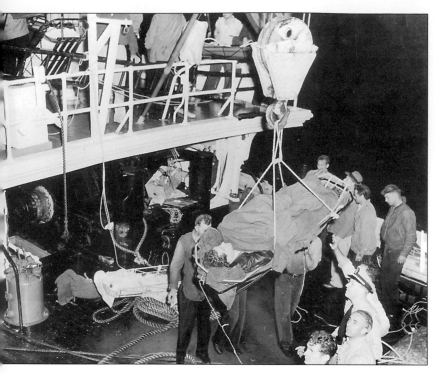

One of 40 rescue vessels sent to the scene of the *Benevolence* collision with the freighter *Mary Luckenbach* takes survivors ashore. *SFMM*

U.S.S. *John W. Thomason* DD-760, a San Francisco-based destroyer, responds to the call for assistance from the sinking hospital ship. *Author's Collection*

Three years later, on June 25, 1950, North Korea invaded its neighbor, South Korea, and the United States was drawn into the first war in support of the United Nations. Initially, the war was not going well for the United Nations. With casualties mounting at an unprecedented rate, there was again an immediate need for hospital ships.

Recommissioning and Sea Trials

The *Benevolence* was selected for reactivation as she was available in the San Francisco Reserve Fleet Group and could be refitted at the nearby Mare Island Naval Shipyard. Removing her from her "mothballed" state was accomplished quickly, and by early August 1950, the hospital ship was ready for sea trials. The Navy literally rushed the *Benevolence* into service and by August 10, the United Nations was asked to notify the North Korean government that the hospital ship would be operating off their coastline and was a designated noncombatant vessel. The final aspect of reactivation included a series of routine tests off the Golden Gate, and when satisfied that the ship was in all respects ready for sea, it was to be turned over to the Military Sea Transport Service. There was such a vital need for the services that could be provided by a hospital ship that the late August tests were conducted with both naval and prospective civilian crews aboard, including military medical staffs. When she embarked for her final sea trials, 526 people were aboard, and in the haste to get the ship to sea, headquarters ashore was not notified of her full roster of personnel. There was so much anxiety over having the ship sail to the war zone that workers from Mare Island also accompanied the civilian and Navy crews to make instant repairs.

The Collision and Sinking

Having satisfied the Navy that the *Benevolence* was ready for sea, the ship was on her way back to San Francisco to discharge her Navy crew and pick up the remainder of her cargo and provisions. On the afternoon of August 25, 1950, a thick fog, common to the coastal area off the Golden Gate, set in and visibility was reduced to less than 100 feet. The *Benevolence*, still under the command of Captain Barton E. Bacon Jr., USN, was making her way into the main ship channel leading into San Francisco Bay. At the helm was Captain Lyle G. Havens, a certified harbor pilot, and the radar scope was manned. Although there were five targets visible on radar, no ships or other potential hazards were deemed as threats to the hospital ship. As she entered the main ship channel, she was making 18 knots or nearly flank speed.

At approximately 5 P.M., the *Mary Luckenbach*, a 15,000-ton Luckenbach Steamship Company general cargo freighter, loomed out of the fog 50 yards off the port bow of the

U.S.S. *Buck* DD-761 joined the *Thomason* in the search for survivors. Ironically, these two ships collided off Korea just months after the loss of the *Benevolence*. The *Buck* was badly damaged and had to return to the West Coast for repairs. *Author's Collection*

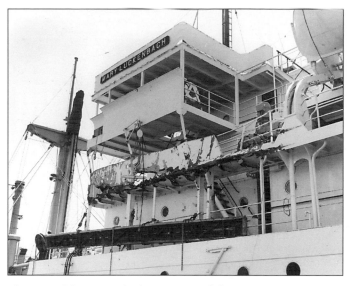

The port side upper deck structure of the *Mary Luckenbach* shows the damage sustained while scraping along the hull of the *Benevolence*. SFMM

Benevolence. She was making 6–8 knots and, although the engine room quickly was instructed to reverse engines, she plowed into the *Benevolence* just forward of the bridge on the port side. Captain Havens attempted to take evasive action and ordered full stop, but it was too late. The hospital ship reeled under the impact and, as she regained stability, the freighter again struck and bumped along her port side. The *Mary Luckenbach* then drifted 500 yards astern where she anchored.

Aboard the now stricken *Benevolence* there was little panic, as discipline surmounted fear. She had been mortally wounded and would founder within 20 minutes. She had been holed beneath the waterline in a number of locations, and there was little time to do anything except send out an SOS. The guard radio at the Treasure Island Naval Station picked up her call at 5:04 P.M. and within minutes Coast Guard and naval units were on their way to the scene of the disaster. The *Benevolence* began to list to port and dip slowly forward as water now freely coursed through her compartments. Men and women poured up from below and in lieu of an "abandon ship" order began to don lifejackets and launch lifeboats. Many now hung on as the ship first listed 45 degrees; at 70 degrees, most either jumped or scaled down her sloping side into the frigid waters. The crew was able to launch a few lifeboats and most rafts were quickly filled. Fog intensified the difficulty for rescue units and although the ship's foghorn continued to sound an SOS, it appeared that no one was going to respond. At approximately 5:20 P.M., amidst a boiling effect as air escaped from the hull, the *Benevolence* rolled over on her port side in 75 feet of water. Survivors could plainly see her red cross insignia, and rigging protruded above water. Many of her lifeboats drifted away from hundreds of survivors that struggled in the water. Help was on the way, but the fog presented a real problem.

The Rescue and Aftermath

The *Mary Luckenbach* sat anchored less than a mile from the now sunken hospital ship and ironically did little to assist the victims. Her captain presumed that the hospital ship had survived with minor damage and had then proceeded to San Francisco. Interestingly, Captain Leonard Smith of the *Mary Luckenbach* did not radio a distress message or report of the collision. Eventually, boats were launched from the freighter and they returned with a few survivors that were drifting close by.

Various commercial fishing vessels, such as the *Flora, Angle Frances,* and *San Domingo,* heard the SOS, and along with 40 other craft sped to recover the survivors. Army tug LT 815 arrived quickly and began to haul in swimmers as did Coast Guard cutters including the *Gresham.* Navy destroyers U.S.S. *Thomason* DD-761 and U.S.S. *Buck* DD-760 also joined in the search for survivors. Nearly everything that could float came out of San Francisco Bay that night to assist in the overall rescue effort. One of the commercial fishing boats, the *Flora,*

Bow and stern view of the *Mary Luckenbach* as she is settled in dry dock for repairs. Her fore peak was flooded, but this did not affect her 9,000-ton cargo. *SFMM*

The damage to the upper bow and stern is evident on the *Mary Luckenbach* as the freighter is warped alongside a pier just after the collision. *SFMM*

dumped its valuable load of fish in favor of bringing in 70 swimmers. As soon as a boat was full, it brought the living and dead to Fort Mason and other nearby docking areas.

Rescue boats and ships slowly moved through a huge floating debris field as hundreds of items floated up from the now lost *Benevolence*. It was important to rescue all of the living within two hours as this was the outside time limit for survival in those frigid waters. The rescuers combed the waters all night and into the next morning looking for survivors. The fact that there was not an accurate count of those who had been aboard the ship hampered their efforts. Finally, late in the morning of August 26, rescue workers located the last two survivors. Two officers were found alive on an upturned lifeboat 5 miles out to sea. They were indeed fortunate, but not so fortunate were the 18 dead and scores of injured.

Hospitals ashore took in all of the injured and within weeks most were discharged and back on duty.

The *Mary Luckenbach* entered dry dock on August 28, 1950, for repairs. The freighter had taken some damage to her bow and the port side of her bridge required some minor repair. The overall damage to the *Mary Luckenbach* was slight compared to the loss of 18 lives and a fully equipped hospital ship.

A court of inquiry was held later but the results were inconclusive. *The Mary Luckenbach* should have been sounding her foghorn and her radar should have been monitored. Captain Bacon, on the other hand, was going too fast in fog-shrouded waters. Despite the fact that his radar did not recognize the presence of danger, dependency on radar was no excuse for common-sense precautions.

For two years, the *Benevolence* lay on her side, and at low tide, her white hull and red cross insignia were ominous reminders that the sea is unforgiving. In 1952, her hulk, declared a hazard to navigation, was blown up in a spectacular explosion. Now all that remains are twisted steel frames and plates 8 fathoms under the Pacific.

The bow and upper forward deck of the *Mary Luckenbach*. No one aboard the freighter was killed or injured in the collision. *SFMM*

The overturned hull of the *Benevolence* off the Golden Gate. It served as a mute but dramatic reminder of the dangers inherent at sea. *TIM*

U.S.S. *Belknap* CG-26 and U.S.S. *John F. Kennedy* CV-67
Collision During Night Flying Operations

Carrier–escort collisions during flight operations are one of the most prevalent accidents at sea. The probability of this type of accident is greatly enhanced during night operations as is the overall damage to the ships and loss of personnel. On the evening of November 22, 1975, the missile cruiser U.S.S. *Belknap* CG-26 collided with the U.S.S. *John F. Kennedy* CV-67 in the Ionian Sea 68 miles east of Sicily. The result was predictable. The *Belknap* was very nearly destroyed and the carrier emerged with minor damage. This was not the first accident of this nature nor will it be the last. In the late night of April 26, 1952, the U.S.S. *Hobson* DMS-26 was literally run over by the carrier U.S.S. *Wasp* CV-18 and sliced in half. Both halves of the destroyer minesweeper quickly sank with 176 of her 237-man crew. Most were asleep and died immediately. Similarly, the destroyer U.S.S. *Frank E Evans* DD-754 was cut in half by the Australian aircraft carrier

Melbourne R-21 on June 2, 1969, while on exercises in the early morning hours. In less than two minutes the bow section containing 74 men slid under the Pacific. In both instances the primary blame rested on destroyer officers who were not fully attentive to the hazards of operating in close quarters with fast ships that are many times larger and less responsive.

Small cruisers, destroyers, and frigates act as escorts for the fast carriers and also provide plane guard service. During flight operations, escorts are stationed at critical locations near the carrier to pick up downed pilots. The ongoing problem for small ship watch standers is to have their vessel in the right place at the right time. The carrier is a prisoner of the wind and must turn into it to launch and recover aircraft. This means that the escorts are required to quickly negotiate their way to a new station to fulfill their obligation in flight operations. Anticipating carrier direction changes is an art and often an escort posts someone to continuously observe the carrier in order to begin an evolution prior to last-minute notice. Frequently, an escort is required to pass in front of the accelerating carrier in order to take up its new

The missile cruiser U.S.S. *Belknap* CG-26 after being rebuilt in the 1980s. Now she mounts a Vulcan Phalanx 20-millimeter CIWS for close-in defense; the 3-inch/50-caliber guns have been removed. *Author's Collection*

The supercarrier U.S.S. *John F. Kennedy* CVA-67 at sea. Although a direct descendent of the first supercarrier, U.S.S. *Forrestal* CVA-59, the *Kennedy* had so many improvements she was in a class of her own. *Author's Collection*

Sister ship U.S.S. *Fox* CG-33 in the same configuration as the *Belknap* on the night she collided with the *John F. Kennedy*. *Author's Collection*

station. Extreme care is required during this type of execution, and failure can mean the loss of a ship and personnel as in the case of the *Hobson*.

On the night of November 22, 1975, the *Kennedy* was operating in a part of the Mediterranean known as the Ionian Sea, approximately 68 miles from Sicily. Her task group included escorts U.S.S. *Claude V. Ricketts* DDG-5, U.S.S. *Dale* CG-19, U.S.S. *Bordelon* DD-881, and a number of frigates. The *Kennedy* prepared to recover aircraft and notified the escorts of her intended movements. As aircraft were inbound and probably low on fuel, the crews had to carry out the evolution quickly and efficiently.

The Belknap *and the* Kennedy *Collide*

The U.S.S. *Belknap*, commissioned on November 7, 1964, was a modern missile cruiser that displaced 7,890 tons full load and was 547 feet in length. Her beam was 54 feet 9 inches, and she was capable of 32 knots on steam turbines that generated 85,950 shaft horsepower. The *Belknap* was armed with a single 5-inch/54-caliber gun, two 3-inch/50-caliber guns, Terrier missiles, ASROC, and antisubmarine (ASW) torpedoes. Much of her superstructure was aluminum or aluminum reinforced to reduce topside weight.

The supercarrier U.S.S. *John F. Kennedy* was commissioned on September 7, 1968, and because she incorporated many updates based on her predecessors, she was considered a class unto herself. She was 1,047 feet in length and displaced 87,000 tons full load. Her maximum speed was 35 knots on 280,000 shaft horsepower. The *Kennedy* could embark up to

105 aircraft but normally carried less than 90. The *Kennedy* was assigned to the Sixth Fleet at the time of the collision.

As the night of November 22, 1975, wore on, the *Kennedy* signaled the escorts that flight operations were to begin soon. The *Belknap* was on station 2,000 yards directly ahead of the carrier and was ordered to proceed to a position aft of the *Kennedy* to rescue any pilots that might crash or bail out during aircraft recovery operations. This was a routine procedure, and the cruiser signaled she would take up her new station. Within moments, however, the cruiser found herself steaming toward the port overhang of the *Kennedy* at the terminus of the canted deck. Incredibly, the *Belknap* avoided being sliced in half; however, her upper superstructure struck the huge flight deck overhang, and the carrier's external aviation fuel lines ruptured. This turned what would have been a simple collision with major upper works damage into an uncontrollable flaming inferno. The aviation fuel rained down on the ship as she bounced alongside the quickly moving carrier. Within 30 seconds the burning ship was clear and far in the wake of the carrier whose returning aircraft sheered away from the disaster.

The U.S.S. *Wasp* CV-18 after colliding with the U.S.S. *Hobson* DMS-26. When the *Wasp* struck the luckless destroyer head-on, the *Hobson* sank within seconds. *Author's Collection*

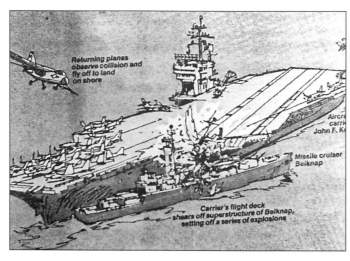

An illustration of what occurred when the *Kennedy* struck the *Belknap*. TIM

Aboard the cruiser, the forward and aft "macks" (combination stack and mast) were sheared off as well as the radar and most of the upper superstructure.

The *Kennedy* did not escape damage and, although minor, a fire broke out on the flight deck edge. The crew extinguished the flame within 10 minutes and the carrier returned to flight operations. One man aboard the *Kennedy* was killed.

Aboard the *Belknap*, however, the damage was substantial. Fifty-five men were forced to jump over the side as the carrier and the destroyer collided. The cruiser drifted away from the

scene on fire from her bridge to the "helo" landing platform aft. Damage control was immediately initiated, but the difficulty was far beyond the capability of those on board the burning ship.

The sea was moderately rough, the winds at 15 knots or more, and occasional rain squalls struck the *Belknap*, which by now was burning furiously. Her aluminum reinforced superstructure literally was melting due to the intense heat; men sought refuge either aft on the fantail or forward on the forecastle. The destroyer *Claude V. Ricketts* was approximately 4 miles distant and immediately steamed toward the flickering ship. Other ships such as the cruiser *Dale* were assigned a variety of tasks ranging from providing medical evacuation to assisting in fire fighting, but it fell to the *Ricketts* to come alongside the *Belknap*. Within minutes, she was coming in off the bow of the *Belknap* and slowly passed by her side until she was abreast of the burning cruiser's stern. Hoses plied hundreds of gallons of seawater onto the crippled ship, and the *Ricketts* stood in even closer despite the danger of exploding 3-inch/50-caliber ammunition that was now cooking off. The fires never reached the 5-inch magazine, the ASW torpedoes, or the Terrier/ASROC magazine up forward—the *Belknap* would have been vaporized if they had. Included within the ship's arsenal were six M-45 nuclear warheads designed for use on the 40-mile-range Terrier missile. Fortunately, there was no radiation leak nor any damage to these weapons.

Twenty hoses were plied on the *Belknap* in either direct stream or fog. The fire came dangerously close to the forward ASW torpedoes and chaff rockets, but at the last minute the sheer amount of water (2,500 gallons per minute) prevented a further tragedy. Had these weapons ignited into any sizable detonation, the Terrier missile and warhead storage magazine up forward would have been threatened.

Aside from fighting fires, 55 men in the water and many wounded aboard the *Belknap* required immediate medical attention. The *Dale* and other escorts provided boats that shuttled the wounded to waiting medical attention. The trips between the burning cruiser and other ships were dangerous due to the high sea state. Within hours boats and helicopters rescued the 55 swimmers. Explosions and flames prevented helicopters from approaching the burning ship, so it was up to the surface ships to provide continuous rescue and fire-fighting services. As the sky began to lighten, the fires were under control and the

The rescue ship, destroyer U.S.S. *Claude V. Ricketts* DDG-5. As with all *Charles F. Adams*-class destroyers, the *Ricketts* has now been decommissioned. *USNI*

The U.S.S. *Bordelon* DD-881, which towed the *Belknap* to Sicily for temporary repairs. *USNI*

Damage to the carrier *John F. Kennedy*. Her external aviation fuel lines ruptured as the cruiser struck her starboard side and fires broke out on both ships. *USNI*

An example of damage the fires caused as they swept the decks and superstructure of the *Belknap*. *USNI*

A view of the incredible damage the *Belknap* sustained. The damage extended from the bridge back to the helicopter deck. *USNI*

blackened mess that was once a beautiful and graceful missile cruiser became discernible. The *Ricketts* remained alongside the *Belknap* and the injured men transferred to it. But it was not yet over. After it appeared that the fires were out or fully contained, a flare-up occurred. The *Belknap* lost all water pressure and it was up to the *Ricketts* to put out the last fires. Finally, the fires were declared defeated and the U.S.S. *Bordelon* came alongside to tow the "cold iron" smoldering ship to Naples, Italy. Another fire flashed, but was put out quickly. The long night was finally over and the *Belknap* began her trip to the Italian mainland behind the *Bordelon*.

Epilogue

One man was killed aboard the *John F. Kennedy* and seven died from the *Belknap*'s crew. Six immediately, and one later due to severe burns. Forty-seven men were injured on the cruiser; 24 of them required extended hospital care. The ship was very nearly declared a constructive loss, but was rebuilt at a huge cost (estimated to be $700 million) and recommissioned on May 10, 1980. Repairs to the *Kennedy* were completed immediately and she was soon operational. Ironically, a similar accident occurred less than a year later when the *Kennedy* collided with the U.S.S. *Bordelon* on September 14, 1976. The 31-year-old destroyer was sufficiently damaged, decommissioned, and later scrapped.

A number of rumors surrounded the true cause of the collision between the *Kennedy* and the *Belknap*, but the Navy eventually found fault with the cruiser's officer of the deck. He was found guilty of negligence and disobedience of orders. Today, the *Belknap* is slated for scrapping, yet 23 years ago she miraculously survived a severe fire. Credit for that rare feat of superb damage control goes to the men aboard the *Belknap* and the *Claude V. Ricketts*.

A beam view of the *Belknap* shortly after the collision; the fires have already been extinguished. The Navy became justifiably concerned about the vulnerability of the aluminum ship construction and the unanticipated extent of fire damage possible. *USNI*

Belknap-class missile cruisers have been retired from the naval service. Here in Suisun Bay, California, a nest of the once sleek and graceful ships awaits their turn under the scrapper's torch. *Author's Collection*

The *Belknap* enters the harbor in Sigonella, Catant, Sicily, for temporary repairs. The Navy revisited the current concept of ship construction and made significant improvements in later cruiser and destroyer classes. *USNI*

U.S.S. *Missouri* BB-63
The "Mighty MO" Hard Aground

One of the most significant warships of the twentieth century is the battleship U.S.S. *Missouri* BB-63. The last battleship completed by the U.S. Navy, her history is replete with momentous national and international events. On her deck, the Allied Nations received the surrender of the Japanese Empire on September 2, 1945, in a ceremony that took a mere 23 minutes to formally end humanity's most horrific world war. Her future assignments included employment in the Korean Conflict and most recently in the 1991 Persian Gulf War. However, an incident in January 1950 caused a great deal of embarrassment to the Navy and could have resulted in the loss of this expensive and notable warship. On January 17, 1950, the world's most powerful battleship ran aground on Thimble Shoals in Chesapeake Bay.

The Battleship U.S.S. Missouri *BB-63: Construction and World War II*

The keel for what would become the U.S.S. *Missouri* was laid on January 6, 1941, 11 months before the United States' entry into World War II. She was built in the New York Navy Yard and launched three years later on January 29, 1944. She is 887 feet 3 inches in length and has a beam of 108 feet 2 inches. Her full load displacement is 57,540 tons and eight Babcock and Wilcox boilers can still provide sufficient steam to her four turbines to generate up to 212,000 shaft horsepower. Her maximum speed is 33 knots. She is well armored with up to 13.5 inches on her sides and 17 inches on the face plates of her main battery turrets. The sides of her citadel are 17.3 inches in thickness and the passage tube from the lower deck is encased by 16 inches of armor.

In 1944, she mounted a main battery of nine 16-inch guns in three turrets, backed up by a secondary battery of 20 5-inch/38-caliber dual purpose guns. The antiaircraft capability was formidable with 80 40-millimeter guns and 49 20-millimeter guns.

The *Missouri* was well suited for task force protection against the swarm attacks of Kamikazes anticipated near the Japanese homeland. On June 11, 1944, the huge bat-

The U.S.S. *Missouri* BB-63 visits Sydney, Australia, in 1987 on a good-will tour. She has been modernized and now carries Tomahawk and Harpoon missiles as well as four Vulcan Phalanx 20-millimeter CIWS for close-in defense. *Author's Collection*

tleship was commissioned and assigned to the Pacific War.

The *Missouri* became an active unit in the Pacific War in early 1945 as part of Task Group 58.2 that included the carrier U.S.S. *Lexington* CV-2 and U.S.S. *Hancock* CV-19 as well as her sister ship, the U.S.S. *Wisconsin* BB-64. They supported the landings on Iwo Jima and then accompanied the fast carrier on strikes on Okinawa and Tokyo. Ironically, the *Wisconsin* acted in concert with the *Missouri* on her final wartime assignment in the 1991 Persian Gulf War.

The *Missouri* provided a powerful antiaircraft battery to the fast carrier task forces, and her AA guns knocked down a number of incoming Kamikazes, the world's first guided missiles. On April 11, 1945, a suicide plane struck the battleship on her hull, but the damage was minimal. Kamikazes primarily targeted the hangar deck elevators aboard the carriers, yet often sought out battleships as a method of dying.

The Pacific War came to a rather abrupt end after the twin atomic bombings of major Japanese cities, and it fell to the *Missouri* to host the surrender activities. In the main, it is believed that the *Missouri* was selected because President Harry Truman (a native of Missouri) wanted it so. Also, his wife had christened the ship. On September 2, 1945, the ceremonies were held ending the most violent and costly war in human history.

Hard Aground: Anatomy of a Shipwreck

In the five years that followed the end of World War II, the *Missouri* carried out a number of assignments, including midshipmen training cruises and flag showing abroad. There was a new conflict brewing simply termed the "Cold War," and the battleship played a very small role in this new phenomenon in international politics. It was a war of words and territorial expansion through the spread of ideology backed up by modern military hardware. Intercontinental ballistic missiles, electronic countermeasures, atomic-bomb-carrying heavy bombers, and the submarine supplanted the battleship even more than the aircraft carrier had during World War II. Keeping battleships in commission was an expensive proposition, and any time that the Navy made an embarrassing mistake, its detractors were quick to point out the foolishness of the American taxpayer having to foot the bill for obsolete military hardware. Those who decried the value of the Navy were given

In an ironic twist, Japanese sailors view and admire the plaque imbedded on the deck of the Missouri that commemorates the surrender of their country to the Allies. *TIM - SFCB*

Quartermaster Bevin E. Travis 2nd Class was at the wheel when the *Missouri* slid onto the mud bank on January 17, 1950. The grounding was not his fault. *TIM - SFCB*

more political ammunition than they ever dreamed of on the morning of January 17, 1950.

It was well known that being assigned the command of a battleship was a step up for a captain that aspired to flag rank. So it was for Captain William D. Brown when he assumed command of one of the most celebrated battleships in the U.S. Navy. He took command on December 10,

The Navy off-loads 16-inch ammunition and other stores onto barges alongside the ship. The object was to lighten the stranded battleship to the greatest extent possible. *TIM - SFCB*

Portable winches attached to the deck of the battleship will pull on cables anchored away from the ship when the "big push/pull" begins. *TIM - SFCB*

The first real attempt to dislodge the stranded ship on January 31, 1950, with a series of tugs is a failure. A greater effort is called for. *TIM - SFCB*

Another view of the failed early morning attempt to free the *Missouri* on January 31, 1950. *TIM - SFCB*

1949, and within a few days the *Missouri* left the Portsmouth Navy Yard for trials off the coast. She returned on December 23, 1949, in time for the crew to have Christmas ashore. The officers and crew began to acclimate themselves to their new commanding officer who, like many, had idiosyncrasies and different methods comparative to the previous captain. Captain Brown was a competent ship handler; however, his experience was limited to small destroyer-type vessels. He also demonstrated a tendency toward micromanagement with a consequent inability to delegate tasks and responsibilities to subordinates.

In early January 1950, the *Missouri* was alerted for duty off Guantanomo Bay, Cuba, where she and a number of other ships would be engaged in annual maneuvers and exercises. Her date of departure from the Norfolk Navy Yard was set for January 17, 1950, after being fully ammunitioned and provisioned. Just prior to her departure, Brown was notified that his new command was to carry out a voluntary collateral mission. It was optional in that Brown could refuse based on operational or other compelling reasons. Since he acknowledged the request, he was to take the *Missouri* through an expressly marked channel near the harbor exit that was strewn with

specially placed acoustic cables. The Navy was attempting to develop a system of identifying ships by their propeller signatures. The battleship would be recorded as she steamed over the cables near Old Point Comfort. The run was charted and the channel prominently marked with buoys.

Unfortunately, two of the five marker buoys indicated on the chart had been removed, and the navigating staff aboard the *Missouri* were unaware of this change. This was but a foreshadowing of a series of errors that always seems to be present in shipping disasters. The *Missouri* left her mooring at 7:25 A.M. and stood out of the harbor under the command of a local pilot. Conning a battleship was far more difficult than a destroyer as Captain Brown would soon discover. The weather presented no problem, and at 7:49 A.M. the harbor pilot bid the giant ship farewell and handed it over to the ship's captain. The *Missouri* carried on toward the test range at a slow but manageable speed. The executive officer, Commander George Peckham, remarked that the ship appeared to be heading toward two red markers that signified shoal waters on the chart. The *Missouri* drew 37 feet, which was far too much for the depth of water near the red warning markers. At 12 minutes after 8 A.M., Captain Brown compounded what was to become

Finally, on February 1, 1950, the great ship is pulled loose using almost all of the salvage resources on the East Coast. *TIM - SFCB*

The *Missouri's* band plays the "Missouri Waltz" to tell its crew that the ship is again afloat. *TIM - SFCB*

28

The crew watches with relief as the *Missouri* is slowly nudged off the mud bank and out into deep water on February 1, 1950. *TIM - SFCB*

An aerial view of the huge effort to free the battleship. The operation included strategically placed tugs to deliver the maximum amount of pressure on the ship—it worked. *TIM - SFCB*

a serious error in communication. He ordered the ship's speed increased to 15 knots so as to give the rudders greater purchase, thus increasing maneuverability. Shortly after the engine speed increase, he was alerted that an orange-and-white marker buoy was ahead. He was then counseled that the ship could pass to the starboard of the buoy when in fact the ship should have kept the buoy to its left. Two spar buoys now appeared off the bow and were assumed to signify the end of the course, yet showed a shoal water depth of 14 feet. Radar readings that also showed danger were ignored. By now, even the helmsman knew that the great ship was in trouble. QM 2nd Class Bevan Travis felt the wheel become sluggish and the ship involuntarily slow down. It was 8:17 A.M. and the *Missouri* had slid up on a mud bar, or shoal, for most of her length. Her black boot top was several feet out of the water at the bow, and the engines had been shut down due to sand clogging her intakes. She was hard aground off Thimble Shoal and in plain view of the shore, the Navy, the media, and her most ardent detractors. It was no longer a question as to whether a disaster had occurred, it was whether the ship would become a permanent fixture (*Missouri* Shoals?) or if she could be quickly refloated in reasonably good condition.

By 8:30 A.M., a request was made that all available tugs be summoned to pull the stranded ship off the mud, which was deferred until the situation could be assessed. Fortunately, salvage resources and the services of one of the great salvage masters were available. Rear Admiral Homer Wallin assumed command of the salvage effort and initiated a five-part plan: Remove all possible weight; provide buoyancy with pontoons; water-jet mud and sand from around the ship; use brute pulling and pushing force; and, finally, dredge a channel for the escape.

Everything possible was brought to bear, including the same pontoons used to raise the sunken submarine U.S.S. *Squalus* SS-192 in 1939. All ammunition, supplies, fuel, and other detachable equipment were removed and the channel dredged. Finally on February 1, 1950, just 17 days after the *Missouri* slid aground, she slid back into deep water with the assistance of 23 vessels. Five tugs pulled alongside, six pulled astern, and three swung the bow to facilitate movement. Two salvage ships were connected astern and seven yard tugs held the other vessels in place. Kedge anchors were out and used as part of the big

Rear Admiral Homer Wallin, the salvage master who freed the ship, points to a 12-foot gash in the hull. An old anchor, left years before buried in the mud under the stranded ship, made the gash. *TIM - SFCB*

Officers and men celebrate as the ship gathers speed and leaves the mud bank shortly after 7 A.M. on the first of February. *TIM - SFCB*

31

pull. There was some difficulty with the hull being held by an old buried anchor, but the salvage team overcame this and towed the *Missouri* to the dry dock formerly occupied by her uncompleted sister ship, the U.S.S. *Kentucky*. Contrary to her detractors who had hoped for serious damage, the *Missouri* was soon fit for sea.

A court of inquiry was held in the wake of this disaster and the blame ultimately fell on the shoulders of Captain Brown and three subordinates. Brown was found guilty of negligence and suffered the loss of 250 numbers on the promotion list. This meant that he would not be promoted while on active duty. Other officers received lesser penalties and the incident was formally closed.

Epilogue

The *Missouri* fought through the Korean War and was subsequently moth-balled at the Puget Sound Naval Shipyard in Bremerton, Washington. In 1985, the 41-year-old battleship was reactivated and modernized with a mixture of Harpoon antiship missiles, Tomahawk cruise missiles, Phalanx CIWS guns, and electronic countermeasures. She went to war again in 1991 against Iraq and fired 759 16-inch projectiles. The turret explosion experience of 1989 aboard the U.S.S. *Iowa* was still very much on the minds of naval ordnance experts and no expense was spared to prevent a reoccurrence of that disaster. New ammunition and trained experts were embarked on the "Mighty MO" for her last appearance as a fighting ship. She also fired 28 missiles at inland targets, yet it was her gun support that ground forces most appreciated.

With the war over, the aging ship made an appearance at the ceremony signifying the 50th anniversary of the Japanese attack on Pearl Harbor, and then went back to Bremerton for

The battleship does what she was built for—fires a nine-gun main battery salvo. To the immediate left, two projectiles can be seen on their way to a target. *Author's Collection*

In a classic pose, the U.S.S. *Missouri* rests at the Puget Sound Naval Shipyard in Bremerton, Washington. In late 1998 her home port will be Pearl Harbor as a war memorial moored near the U.S.S. *Arizona. Author's Collection*

deactivation. In June 1998, she was towed to Hawaii and in mid-1999 will become a part of the Pearl Harbor Memorial.

The 1950 grounding was a disaster, but just one in passing. This incident proved that the Navy is highly adept at salvage. The U.S.S. *Missouri* will not be known for her grounding, but will be remembered for her value to our Navy and nation on the international stage.

Destroyer Squadron 11
The Death of Destroyer Squadron 11

The Armistice ending World War I had been signed nearly five years before a bizarre incident that took the lives of 23 seamen and caused the total loss of seven modern U.S. Navy destroyers valued at $13.5 million. Although the loss of life was less than that experienced in other disasters, the incident involving Destroyer Squadron 11 is still regarded as the worst peacetime naval blunder in U.S. Naval history.

It was September 8, 1923, the time was 9:05 P.M., and within seven minutes the

Delphy DD-261, *Young* DD-312, *S. P. Lee* DD-310, *Woodbury* DD-309, *Nicholas* DD-311, *Chauncey* DD-296, and *Fuller* DD-297 followed one another onto the rocks, shoals, and reefs adjacent to the central California coast. They were not the first, nor would they be the last, to fall victim to this well-known graveyard of ships. In all, 26 major vessels have been stranded, held hostage, or reduced to rusting skeletons at Point Honda.

The Japanese merchantman *Nippon Maru* was impaled on Woodbury Rock (so named for the U.S.S. *Woodbury*) September 1, 1933; the American passenger liner S.S. *Harvard* became hopelessly stranded on May 30, 1931; and the Greek ex-liberty ship *Kulukundis* grounded close by on July 11, 1949. All became total losses.

Today, the area remains dangerous to seafarers due to shifting currents, volcanic-like jagged reefs, and dense fog that shrouds the channel for nearly 25 percent of the year. The area is known as the Devil's Jaw because the vice-like rocks have claimed the lives of so many ships and sailors. On the evening of September 8, 1923, a minor miscalculation caused a major error in judgment, and tragedy resulted.

Flush Deck, Four Piper Destroyers

The U.S. Navy commissioned 267 destroyers as the result of World War I building programs, yet only 39 preceded the Armistice. Many were not even built until after the war, and a large number sailed virtually from commissioning to mothballs (inactive reserve) and eventually to the shipbreakers.

The lead ships were known as the *Wickes* or *Clemson* class and the quality of individual ship construction varied from shipyard to shipyard. The common specifications of the flush deckers were a length of 314 feet 4 inches and a beam of 30 feet 11 inches with a displacement of 1,149 tons. The "four pipers," as they became known, were powered by steam turbines generating 24,610 shaft horsepower, which enabled these ships a healthy 35-plus knots on two shafts. They were armed with four 4-inch/50-caliber guns, torpedoes, depth charges (ASW), and a 3-inch AA battery. In peacetime, their crew totaled 131 officers and enlisted personnel.

Due to the large number of four pipers

available, many were selected for various roles during the interwar years. These ranged from illegal liquor suppression, mine laying, minesweeping, coastal patrol, remote control target ships, seaplane tenders, and training.

Low Power Run from San Francisco to San Diego

Destroyer Squadron 11, under the command of Captain Edward Howe Watson, was in San Francisco Harbor during that city's annual Fleet Week in September 1923. The post-World War I U.S. Navy was under close scrutiny by a public and political system weary of military expenditures. The media watched the military carefully for excessive spending.

The ships of Destroyer Squadron 11 were not exempt from severe budget cuts, and most carried smaller crews than the normal complement necessary to operate on a peacetime basis. There was a strict fuel allotment per ship, and for the upcoming 427-mile run from San Francisco to the destroyer base in San Diego, all ships were required to steam on the two low-power, or cruising turbines at the maximum speed of 20 knots. While a sustained 20-knot speed was possible on the low-power turbines, it was laborious for the engineering plants, and most captains and chief engineers privately disagreed with the practice.

Fourteen four pipers of Destroyer Squadron 11 left San Francisco on September 8, 1923. Five others did not accompany the squadron due to engine problems or being dry-docked.

The steaming formation was that of a single column led by the flagship *Delphy*, on which the squadron commander, Captain Watson rode. The interval between ships was 250 yards, but more to the point, the distance from the stern of one ship to the bow of that following was 147 yards. At 20 knots, a mere 13 seconds separated them. The flagship was responsible for squadron navigation and taking radio direction finder (RDF) bearings from the three new and untried stations on the California coast.

To poor RDF support, a follow-the-leader mentality, no independent navigation by each ship, inexperienced officers, and only 13 seconds separating each vessel was added thick fog, the waiting graveyard of ships, and a minor miscalculation. The miscalculation consisted of the flagship navigator leading the column on a course of 150 degrees and swinging 95 degrees to port too soon. Mistakenly, he felt that the column had entered the Santa Barbara Channel, and to avoid San Miguel Island, he ordered a port turn. He failed to take soundings, reduce speed due to poor visibility, or get a proper fix on the RDF station at Point Arguello (the entrance to the Santa Barbara Channel). Within minutes this error—compounded by circumstance—caused the *Delphy* to slam into the jagged rocks of the Devil's Jaw. It was 9:05 P.M., and thinking that the ship had run aground on San Miguel Island, the *Delphy* signaled the other ships to immediately turn to port or westward to avoid collision. This final judgment error spelled the doom for another six ships as they steered directly for the coast rather than away from it. In rapid succession, they began to tear and grind over the rocks and reefs.

The *S. P. Lee* was next to strike the rocks at 9:06 P.M. The *Young* struck at about the same time, yet she did not remain on an even keel like her sister ship. Within 90 seconds of striking bottom, the *Young* heeled over 90 degrees to starboard. She was immediately flooded, and in desperation the crew abandoned as quickly as possible. Many were asleep and had to abandon with little or no clothing on. In total darkness and confusion, the crew of the *Young* climbed and slid along the port side of the ship, and in the bright glow of a searchlight of another destroyer they were able to gain a perspective of the situation. Many were able to use the portlights as handholds and crawl toward some form of temporary safety. There was no immediate assistance as other ships within a few hundred yards of the *Young*'s position were having difficulties of their own.

Within seconds, the *Woodbury* struck a major surface rock formation about 200 yards from shore and became permanently lodged there. Although the crew and officers were inexperienced, they were successfully able to leave the ship and gain a foothold on what would be named Woodbury Rock in honor of their ship. The *Nicholas* was next. She hit a submerged pinnacle with her starboard propeller and became firmly wedged in the rocks within a few yards of the beach. Her bow was pointing seaward, but there she would remain. Her crew abandoned ship in an orderly manner. Just westward of the *Woodbury*, the *Fuller*, seventh ship in line, struck the outermost edge of the Devil's Jaw and tore substantial holes in her hull. She began to flood and slowly sink.

The *Chauncey*, 10th in line, hit the *Young* with her starboard propeller and tore large gashes in an already doomed ship. The *Chauncey* continued for a few hundred yards and lodged against a low cliff. Part of her aft framework and one boiler remain today among the rocks. Only seven minutes had elapsed since the *Delphy* struck. In that time seven ships were lost and over 700 officers and men were stranded in various locations in dense fog and rough water. Many were injured and by the time they were rescued, 23 had died of injury or drowning. But for the survivors, the terror and misery were just beginning.

Abandonment and Rescue

The other seven destroyers of Squadron 11 did not run aground. The U.S.S. *Farragut* DD-300 and U.S.S *Kennedy* DD-306 struck something, but they were able to extract themselves before any serious damage was done. They stood off out of danger and radioed for help. Assistance from shore was necessary immediately. Unfortunately, the Devil's Jaw is as foreboding on shore as it is at sea, and the nearest possible aid was in a Union Pacific railroad repair and mainte-

The U.S.S. *S. P. Lee* DD-310 makes smoke on a speed run shortly before her end on the night of September 8, 1923. The *Lee* and other ships in the formation were graceful and distinctively American destroyers. *Author's Collection*

nance shed along the Pacific Coast railroad line. John Giorvas, who occupied the maintenance station, noticed the erratic searchlight beams near the mesa. As he made his way to the water's edge, he saw dozens of men emerging from the sea in near-death states. The railroad supervisor summoned nearby communities for help, which arrived within a few hours.

The U.S.S. *Reno* DD-303 leads a column of destroyers down the California coast. She came to the assistance of the steamer *Cuba* and avoided the Devil's Jaw. Another member of Destroyer Squadron 11, the U.S.S. *J. F. Burnes* DD-299, leads another column in the distance. The distance between ships and positions approximates that of September 8, 1923. *Author's Collection*

The grounded U.S.S. *Chauncey* DD-296, with the overturned hull of the U.S.S. *Young* DD-312 just off her stern. The greatest loss of life occurred on the *Young* as she turned over within minutes of running aground. *Author's Collection*

The *Chauncey*, in the extreme foreground, shortly after being grounded. In the distance, the namesake of Woodbury Rock, the U.S.S. *Woodbury* DD-309, is heeled over to port. In the far distance, the mast and pilot house of the U.S.S. *Fuller* DD-297 are just visible. *Author's Collection*

All that currently remains of the U.S.S. *Chauncey* DD-296. She eventually ended up inshore of Woodbury Rock and was driven up near the cliff side. The rocks are jagged, steep, and sharp. Climbing them at night without shoes would have been torturous. *Author's Collection*

Out on the stranded ships, a variety of dramas were being played out as each man attempted to save himself and those near him. There were many acts of heroism, and virtually no panic or disorder. Discipline and seamanship had taken hold.

By late afternoon on September 9, 775 men had been saved—a feat of no small proportion. In light of the massive loss of ships, however, this accomplishment went virtually unnoticed. Of those rescued, 517 men and 38 officers boarded a specially assigned train and traveled southward to San Diego. A cadre of officers and men stayed on the mesa and formed a "wreck patrol" to ward off looters and look for other survivors.

Epilogue and Aftermath

Within a few days of the disaster, the Navy convened a court of inquiry to look into the wreck and its causes. Unfortunately, the inquiry

The U.S.S. *S. P. Lee* DD-310 is in the foreground, and the hull has obviously buckled just forward of the starboard torpedo mount. The U.S.S. *Nicholas* DD-311 has broken in two in the background. *Author's Collection*

Starboard views of the *S. P. Lee* and *Nicholas* some days after the wreck. None of the seven would ever sail, and due to their locations, minimal salvage was possible. *Author's Collection*

A few officers and men set up a "wreck camp" to protect the ships from vandals and sightseers. Later most of the ordnance, including several of the $5,000 torpedoes, were removed. Wind and wave eventually wore down what remained. *Author's Collection*

was done in secret, a tactic that outraged an already suspicious American public. What eventually emerged after a 19-day series of hearings was a recommendation that 11 officers be court-martialed. Captain Watson was charged with culpable inefficiency and negligence, as were Lt. Comdr. Donald Hunter (Captain) and Lt. (jg) Lawrence F. Blodgett (navigator and executive officer) of the *Delphy*. For negligence, eight other officers were charged.

38

A monument erected to the seven ships and 23 seamen who lost their lives on that foggy September night. Few people visit the area, but the curious can arrange tours through the Public Affairs Office of Vandenberg Air Force Base. *Author's Collection*

The principal culprit in the disaster was the age-old naval procedure of "follow the leader." The *Delphy* was responsible for squadron navigation and all other ships blindly followed, yet when disaster struck, those who followed were charged with negligence! It was, and in some cases still is, the classic military paradox, and the lesson is simple—avoid disaster. Of course there were mitigating circumstances such as fog, high speed, lack of correct RDF bearings, and failure to take basic precautions such as depth soundings. Overconfidence, or the "hairy chest attitude" of reckless bravery, was the final overriding element that ensured disaster.

The verdict of the final court-martial was that Captain Watson and Lt. Comdr. Hunter were guilty as charged. The navigator, Lt. (jg) Blodgett was found not guilty as were the eight other officers, who were exonerated.

Back at the wrecks, one of the unsung heroes was Chief Warrant Officer Morris Hoffman, nicknamed "Fish." He and his Navy dive team recovered 18 bodies and much of the armament including 12 of the 4-inch deck guns and the ships' safes. Forty-four of the $5,000 torpedoes were also retrieved. Morris trained the torpedo tubes seaward and fired the torpedoes to a waiting recovery ship. None of the ships was salvageable, and they were struck from the Navy's active list on November 20, 1923. On October 19, 1925, a salver, Robert Smith of Oakland, bought the wrecks. They were too far gone or inaccessible for any substantial equipment or metal removal, and the hulls were left to wind and wave.

U.S.S. *Milwaukee* Cruiser No. 21
A $7 Million Comedy of Errors

The U.S.S. *Milwaukee* C-21 was one of three cruisers of the *St. Louis* class laid down in early 1902. None would ever find fame in war, and all became submarine tenders for the U.S. Navy's emerging undersea force. The *St. Louis* and sister ship *Charleston* ended their days in the backwaters of naval operations, but on January 13, 1917, the *Milwaukee* went aground on a sandy beach near Eureka, California. She was the victim of inexperience and an amateur approach to salvage. The eventual cost to the Navy was over $7 million and the incident made a laughingstock of its leaders.

U.S.S. Milwaukee: A St. Louis-Class Cruiser

The *St. Louis* class of lightly armored cruisers was a follow-on to the early *Pennsylvania* class of armored cruisers that Congress had authorized in 1899. The new class, however, displaced 4,000 tons less—sufficient to render them poorly armored and weakly armed.

The *Milwaukee* and her sister ships displaced 9,700 tons and were 424 feet in length with a maximum beam of 66 feet. She could steam at 22.13 knots (maximum) from power delivered to two screws from coal-fired, triple expansion engines rated at 27,264 shaft horsepower. She had a draft of 22.5 feet, which was generally unimportant until her adventure near Samoa Beach in Northern California.

The *Milwaukee* mounted 14 6-inch/50-caliber rapid fire guns, 18 3-inch, 12 3-pounders, 8 1-pounders, and 4 30-caliber machine guns. She was designed to carry a crew complement of 36 officers and 627 enlisted men, but generally the number was much smaller as the result of stringent naval appropriations from a congress bent on saving taxpayer dollars.

The cruiser was laid down at the Union Iron Works in San Francisco on July 30, 1902; launched on September 10, 1904; and finally commissioned on December 10, 1906. By March 1908, the extent of her career as a bona fide cruiser was over and she went into reserve. There she remained until June 17, 1913, when she was brought out of storage and reconditioned for fleet reserve work. In mid-1916, the *Milwaukee* found herself at the Mare Island

The submarine *H-3* or *Garfish* shortly after grounding in the surf of Samoa Beach near Eureka, California. A month later the cruiser *Milwaukee* would join her in a farcical salvage attempt. *TIM - SFCB*

Naval Shipyard for a stint in dry dock and a major conversion to a submarine tender. Near the end of this refit, the cruiser was first considered for collateral duty as a salvage ship. The U.S. Navy submarine U.S.S. *H-3* had run aground near Eureka, California, and a stout vessel with massive horsepower was needed on the scene to pull her free.

The U.S.S. H-3 *and the Graveyard of the Pacific*

The *H-3* was built by the Moran Company of Seattle, Washington, and launched on July 3, 1913. Like her sisters, she was a modern submersible, but her interior was wet, clammy, and stank from diesel oil, human sweat, and battery acid. It was not a life for the squeamish or faint of heart. The submarine sail, or open conning tower, stood less than 12 feet above the deck surface. From the waterline, the highest part of the conning tower, exclusive of the periscope, was less than 20 feet.

The general area in and around Humboldt Bay, including the sand dunes and tide flats that border Samoa Beach, had claimed the hulls of 27 ships by the time the U.S.S. *H-3* appeared in the surf 4 miles north of the Bay. Fog and smoke from local lumber mills often shrouded this area, which was renowned for heavy surf conditions, contrary currents, and cold, choppy and unpredictable sea conditions.

Desperate for any point of reference, the submarine's bridge watch searched for the entrance to the bay. Finally, with a sense of relief, one of the lookouts shouted that he could see smoke. The smoke was actually hovering above the Hammond sawmill smokestack which, unfortunately for the *H-3,* was located on land. The noise of the laboring diesel muffled the sound of the surf, and the sand dunes beyond the surf line blended with the sea, causing an illusion for the fog-shrouded lookouts aboard the sub. Within seconds, the *H-3* ran aground and continued forward until her bulk was literally ground into the sand.

The topside watch, including the captain, retreated below and sent out an urgent SOS. The seas were now breaking over her with abandon and her electrical system failed. Now it was up to anyone who might be on the beach to see the stricken sub and have the good sense to report the grounding to the Coast Guard. Three boys who were in the vicinity on their way to school ran to class with the news. The teacher instructed the excited boys to run to the Hammond Lumber Company office and use their telephone to contact the U.S. Coast Guard Humboldt Bay Life Saving Station (Samoa Beach Unit).

The Coast Guard lifesaving crew was professional and, after sizing up the situation, determined that a seaward approach was too dangerous and would unnecessarily risk lives. Instead, a Lyle Line Throwing Gun was set up on the beach. The Coast Guard used this device to throw a messenger line seaward to stranded shipwrecks to set up a breeches buoy for rescue. One of the sub's crew who emerged from the conning tower snagged the first line, but it soon parted due to the severe rolling of the boat. The stranded submariner reentered the conning tower hatch for shelter.

The Coast Guardsmen made a second shot from the beach, but this time no one appeared from the hatch. The guardsmen shot a third that Chief Gunners Mate Jack Agraz made fast, but the block and tackle became fouled and the guardsmen could not use the breeches buoy. It was now after 3 P.M. and the crew of the submarine had been buffeted unmercifully for nearly seven hours in what they hoped would not be their coffin. The guardsmen decided to launch a boat despite the heavy surf. The guardsmen trundled out the surf boat, specifically constructed for this contingency, and allowed it to float free to face the incoming waves. A submariner finally secured the boat to the sub, and one by one the green-faced, bruised submariners came ashore via the breeches buoy. The *H-3* was temporarily left to the elements.

Salvage of the H-3: How Difficult Could It Be?

When the headiness of the grounding and successful rescue of the crew wore off, the crew of the submarine and the U.S. Navy were still faced with the fact that one of their newest submarines was firmly stuck in Samoa Beach sand. It had to be salvaged, and then a minor overhaul would make the boat as good as new.

The coastal monitor and *H-3*'s mother ship, U.S.S. *Cheyenne*, and an ocean-going tug, U.S.S. *Iroquois*, made the first attempt to pull the beached submarine back to sea. It was none too soon as the *H-3* was slowly burrow-

ing into the sand and would eventually disappear. Ten-inch manila hawsers were connected and when December tides were judged highest, a strain was taken by both ships with the *Iroquois* in the lead. Their combined efforts only served to raise the sodden hawser from the surf and twist the broadside-lying submarine a few feet. The *H-3* spent Christmas 1916 firmly embedded in the sand of Samoa Beach. It appeared that this job was going to require a greater commitment of resources.

The U.S.S. Milwaukee Trades Places with the H-3

The Mercer-Fraser Company, a lumber firm in Eureka, approached the Navy with a plan to jack up the sub like a house and transport her over land to the bay. The cost was a mere $18,000, but the Navy scoffed at this plan. After all, the sub was still just a sub and a ship like the modern 9,700-ton, 24,000-horsepower cruiser *Milwaukee* could pull the boat free with ease. Lieutenant W. F. Newton would be in command of the overall expedition, but ironically, no one in the expedition was familiar with large-scale salvage.

By January 12, 1917, the *Milwaukee* was within sight of the wreck as were the *Iroquois* and *Cheyenne*. The simple salvage plan only

The new semiarmored cruiser U.S.S. *Milwaukee* on speed and builders trials in San Francisco Bay shortly after being fitted with her two coal-fired steam engines. The *Milwaukee* and her sisters *Charleston* and *St. Louis* never really were cast in the role of combat cruisers and spent the bulk of their short-lived careers in mundane assignments. *TIM - SFCB*

Boats row in from the now stranded cruiser. The crowds ashore were vindicated in their opinion of the foolhardy salvage attempt. *TIM - SFCB*

required superb seamanship, the cooperation of Mother Nature, and vast quantities of luck. The townspeople, local fishermen, and the Coast Guard disagreed with the plan and, even up to the point when the *Milwaukee* began tugging at the *H-3*, pleaded with Newton to abandon the effort. Their rationale was basic: The *Milwaukee* was too close to the shoreline, sands shifted overnight, and a strong current spelled doom for any ship that close to Samoa Beach.

In theory, the *Milwaukee* would be tethered by cable to one of her escorts in four locations: one off her bow and three off her starboard quarter. Her starboard anchor was set several hundred yards seaward—unfortunately it was on a sandy bottom with poor holding capability. Next, a line was run to the *Cheyenne*; a second anchor again set in sand; and finally, almost parallel to the starboard bow, a cable to the *Iroquois*. Fundamentally, the *Milwaukee* would pull the *H-3* from her sand burrow and her anchors would prevent the cruiser from inadvertently closing the beach. When set, the *Milwaukee* was to be in a minimum of 42 feet depth and 1,600 feet from the first line of breakers. The bow pointing seaward was to be in 48 feet of water and as the cruiser drew 22 feet, the margin was considered safe. This presumed that unusually large breakers would not create a trough of less than 22 feet.

By midafternoon on January 12, 1917, all was in readiness, including a line attached to the stranded submarine. Steel cables of 5 and 6 inches in circumference were eventually secured to the bow of the *H-3* and out to the *Milwaukee* where they were attached to the armor plating of one of the stern's 6-inch guns. The target time for the "big pull" was 3 P.M. on January 13, 1917. Thousands of sightseers had arrived from miles around for this event, most predicting disaster. At the appointed time, all engines were advanced to full and propellers began to kick up quite a froth in the water. A dense fog now shrouded the rescue fleet and, to make matters worse, the line from the *Milwaukee* to the *Cheyenne* was severed by the smaller ship's propeller. She surged away from the struggling cruiser and ultimately to the safety of open sea. At 3:42 P.M. the *Milwaukee's* rudder struck the bottom and, not having a proper point of reference due to fog, the huge cruiser was now perilously close to the shore. Aboard the cruiser, shock and that sickening feeling of being helpless in the face of disaster replaced bravado, and most of the crew were aft watching a catastrophe in the making. It was unbelievable to the Navy, but on the beach a silent chorus of, "I told you so" was certainly on the lips of anyone remotely familiar with local sea conditions. The *H-3* had become her anchor and in a twist of irony pulled the cruiser to her rather than the other way around.

By ten minutes after four, the *Milwaukee* was broadside to the shore with a 20-degree list to port. Breakers and swells literally lifted her up, slammed her down on the bottom,

The cruiser *Milwaukee* lies 300 yards from the shoreline in 12 feet of water on January 14, 1917. Foolish and stubborn pride caused this great ship to become a total loss. Her crew of 438 men had abandoned her the day before. *TIM - SFCB*

The *H-3* being trundled over the sand dunes to Humboldt Bay where she was refloated four months after being stranded. The salvage cost was $18,000 for the Mercer-Fraser Lumber Company to lift the submarine on a sled and drag it back to water. The overall cost of the operation was $7,018,000, which included the loss of a first-class cruiser! *TIM - SFCB*

The cruiser *Milwaukee*, still flying its battle ensign from its main mast, lies at a 20-degree list to starboard. Salvage crews built a trestle to the wreck and then brought in railroad cars. The crews employed a heavy crane to lift off valuable equipment and machinery. *TIM - SFCB*

A classic view of the stricken cruiser from the dunes of Samoa Beach, when she still rode majestically high in the water on a straight keel. This pose soon ended as winter storms swept through and broke her back. Then she was just another wreck in the graveyard of ships. *TIM - SFCB*

and ushered her closer to the shoreline. As she was listing 20 degrees, launching her boats to save the crew was nearly impossible. A breeches buoy was established and men began the long transit from the now hopelessly foundered cruiser to the beach. The breeches buoy took too long so surf boats were added to the rescue effort. The good citizenry of Eureka prepared bonfires and provided coffee, food, blankets, and whiskey. Much of the latter flowed freely and what should have been considered a tragedy became a celebration of the saving of 438 souls. Yet the reality was that the *Milwaukee*

The *Milwaukee* is now just a shipwreck attached to a trestle bridge. Her back is broken and the hulk slowly sinks into the sand. This is how she looked for another quarter century until another war brought further demands on her remains. Scrap hunters reduced her to deck level, taking all available metals for the war effort. *TIM - SFCB*

was no longer a viable fleet unit and now served as a tourist and scavenger magnet.

The next order of business was for the Navy to admit failure and allow the Mercer-Fraser Lumber Company to proceed with their bizarre but effective salvage of the *H-3*. By April 17, 1917, the little submarine was again seaborne in Humboldt Bay. It had taken her four months to reach her original destination, but she was practically unharmed and with the exception of her sheared-off cruising bridge the *H-3* was ready for sea. It was easy and only cost $7,018,000: $18,000 for the submarine salvage contract and $7 million for the lost cruiser and consequent salvage operation.

The U.S.S. Milwaukee: *Hard Aground*

The Navy was faced with a 400-foot-long, 10,000-ton ship rolling in the surf just 300 yards from the shoreline, so a contract was signed with the Mercer-Fraser Company to build a sturdy wooden trestle out to the stricken cruiser. The Northwestern Pacific Railroad would lay track, and active salvage of the ship's "guts" and armaments could begin. The salvage crew mounted a heavy-duty crane, which could lift and deposit gun barrels and other major pieces of machinery directly into waiting rail cars.

Camp Milwaukee was established as a temporary base for personnel attached to the salvage command and as the months went by, the crew removed and shipped out thousands of tons of machinery, ordnance, and supplies. Some of the 6-inch guns later found employment aboard other warships.

The *Milwaukee* was decommissioned on March 6, 1917, and during a fierce storm in November 1918 the once proud ship broke in two. Finally, on August 5, 1919, the remainder of the cruiser was sold to San Francisco businessman I. Schneider for $3,000.

Today, only small remnants remain visible. Incredibly, over two-thirds of the Milwaukee still exists, but those parts are buried in the sand. Someday, during one of the storms that hit Samoa Beach, she will reemerge and people will get a look at a perfect example of an early-twentieth-century warship. Then the story of the $7 million tragic comedy of errors will be told again.

Visitors can still see five pieces of the cruiser on Samoa Beach at low tide. Under the sand lies two-thirds of the 10,000-ton cruiser that may someday emerge. *Author's Collection*

U.S.S. *West Point* AP-23
*Cut Loose and Abandoned
in the Canary Islands*

On January 18, 1994, the S.S. *American Star*, formerly the U.S.S. *West Point* AP-23, drifted aground on the west coast of Fuerteventura Island in the Canary Islands. There her broken hulk remains, slowly disintegrating under the pounding of wind and waves. A tug was towing the one-time pride of the United States Lines and one of the most celebrated U.S. Navy troopships in World War II to Phuket, Thailand, where in her last incarnation the 35,400-ton ship was to be outfitted as a five-star floating hotel.

Heavy weather often causes towlines between major vessels and seagoing tugs to break. In November 1947 the battleship U.S.S. *New Mexico* BB-40 was slipped from her towline but recovered hours later when the weather subsided. Not so lucky were the new owners of the British battleship H.M.S. *Warspite* when she broke her tow off Cornwall in April 1947 and drifted ashore, never to move again. Tragedy would strike again and see the S.S. *American Star* suffer a similar fate.

The Origin of the S.S. America *and the U.S.S.* West Point *AP-23*

In October 1937, the Newport News Shipbuilding and Drydock Company was awarded the contract to build the S.S. *America*, which was to be the successor to the S.S. *Leviathan* of the United States Lines. The *Leviathan* was from an earlier technological generation and operating costs had become prohibitive. The U.S. government subsidized construction costs of the new ship under the auspices of the newly formed Maritime Commission (MC). On August 22, 1938, the S.S. *America* (MC hull #1) was laid down and launched on August 31, 1939. She became the flagship of the United States Lines on August 22, 1940, just two years to the day from having her keel laid. The S.S. *America* was a beautiful and sleek-looking ship with a 723-foot length, and a beam of 93 feet 3 inches. Her full load tonnage was 35,400 and her top speed was 22.5 knots. Up to 1,202 passengers could be embarked in one of three classes of comfort with a crew of over 600, including hotel staff. Unfortunately, World War II intervened, and her intended passenger track across the North Atlantic was no longer safe. In essence, she was all dressed up with no place to go.

The S.S. *America* soon after entering service as the flagship of the United States Lines. Her country of origin and U.S. flags are painted on the hull as a precaution. The United States was still neutral and well-defined markings helped to prevent German U-boats from accidentally sinking her. *USNI*

The U.S.S. *West Point* AP-23 in military markings. She is armed with four 5-inch guns and a small number of antiaircraft weapons. *USNI*

The *West Point* in dry dock in the San Francisco Naval Shipyard during World War II. She was the largest troop transport in U.S. Navy service. *Author's Collection*

The new ship was placed in service as a pleasure cruiser to the West Indies and California. She followed these routes until May 1941, when the United States Lines was ordered to make her available to the U.S. Navy as a troop transport. By June 15, Norfolk Navy Shipyard had converted the ship and repainted it in Navy gray. She was commissioned as one of the Navy's first large transports. She mounted four 5-inch and four 3-inch guns with a small number of 50-caliber machine guns for antiaircraft defense. Her Navy crew was 969 men and she was now able to carry 5,000 fully equipped soldiers. At one point late in her wartime career, the *West Point* carried an incredible 9,305 people, including crew, and had the largest capacity of any U.S. Navy troop transport in World War II.

Just before the United States' entry into World War II in December 1941, the *West Point*, along with a number of other troop ships (U.S.S. *Wakefield* AP-21 and U.S.S. *Leonard Wood* AP-25), was selected to deliver a large contingent of British troops to Bombay, India, to reinforce Commonwealth Forces. Japanese land forces were systematically reducing British defenses on the Malay Peninsula and their aircraft had air superiority in the region. The *West Point* and other transports were later diverted to Singapore, which was experiencing one air attack after another. By late afternoon on January 30, 1942, as Japanese artillery pounded the docks, the *West Point* got underway with 1,276 evacuees consisting of military dependents, naval officers, pilots, and dockyard civilian workers. They made it to Colombo Harbor in Ceylon without major incident but were then rerouted to Bombay, India, to disembark their passengers. By this time, the entire region was under continuous Japanese air and naval attack. Many Allied warships that had accompanied the *West Point*, such as the cruiser H.M.S. *Exeter* and destroyers H.M.S. *Encounter* and H.M.A.S. *Vampire*, were lost within days after escorting the big transport. It was just by fortune that the *West Point* was able to avoid being sunk by Japanese submarines and carrier aircraft. For the next two years she carried troops to various locations in the Pacific and then was rerouted to the Atlantic and Mediterranean for duty transport-

The *West Point* enters New York Harbor with thousands of grateful GIs home from the war in Europe. *USNI*

ing troops, wounded personnel, Red Cross workers, USO entertainers, and, ultimately, Axis prisoners of war. Often troops that embarked in the United States were boarded from trains with blacked-out windows through enclosed piers at night. Security, especially in the early stages of the war, was tight. Men were told they were going to the South Pacific and were outfitted accordingly. After the *West Point* cleared the harbor, the troops were surprised to learn that they were on their way to Southampton, England.

At the conclusion of World War II, the *West Point* ferried U.S. troops home from the European theater as part of the worldwide "magic carpet" operation. In late 1945, the *West Point* was transferred to the Pacific theater where she continued until February 1946. She was decommissioned and subsequently struck from the active Navy list on March 12, 1946. The ex-luxury liner had carried over 350,000 troops during her five years of service plus countless civilians to all areas of the world.

S.S. America: *Back into Commercial Service*

In mid-1946, the *West Point* was returned to the Newport News Shipyard for conversion back to a commercial passenger liner. On November 10, 1946, the newly refurbished liner sailed for Southampton, England, and for the next 18 years maintained a transatlantic cruising schedule. However, by 1958, jet airliners were taking their toll and for the first time, aircraft carried more passengers than the ships 35,000 feet below them. The S.S. *America* was now obsolete and could not compete against air travel or even her larger sister ship the S.S. *United States*. She was sold for $6.3 million to the Chandris Lines, which was owned and operated by a Greek company. That company was shrewd enough to land an exclusive contract from the Australian government to carry immigrants from Europe and the United States to Australia. For the next 14 years, the aging liner transported thousands of men, women,

49

An advertisement for the new Chandris Lines' S.S. *Australis. Steven Tacey*

A flattering painting of the *Australis* before she was bounced back and forth from one owner after another in the 1980s. *Steven Tacey*

and children who wanted a change of lifestyle in Australia. As long as the ship, now christened the S.S. *Australis*, was deemed safe and met common standards of cleanliness, she continued in service. Ultimately, however, the immigrant boom came to an end, and the 34-year-old ship was taken out of service.

Within months, she was purchased by the America Cruise Lines (subsequently renamed Venture Cruise Lines) and resumed her name of S.S. *America*. This business venture soon failed, and for $1 million, the Chandris Lines again owned the ship. This time she was named the S.S. *Italis* and placed in service carrying passengers on Mediterranean cruises. Her silhouette was now changed dramatically with the loss of the forward funnel. When built, the original S.S. *America* had two funnels, with the forward stack being a dummy. This type of naval architecture is not uncommon. The illusion of power and stability is enhanced with more than one funnel (for example, only three of the four funnels mounted on the R.M.S. *Titanic* worked). Chandris Lines had little success with the old ship as did two later owners. She was subsequently known as the *Noga* (1980) and the *Alferdoss* (1984–1993). The Chaophraya Development and Transport Company finally purchased her and she became the S.S. *American Star*. Her new owners paid a hefty $2 million for the ship and an additional $1.5 million to Hellenic Shipyards in order to prepare her for the long trip to Thailand. For nearly two and a half months the dry-docked *American Star* underwent various inspections supervised by the American Bureau of Shipping. Of particular interest was the ultrasound examination of the hull to determine her future seaworthiness and ability to withstand what was estimated to be a 100-day tow job. Finally, in late 1993, the *American Star*, now officially certified for 12 more years of safe service, was ready for her final voyage.

The Final Voyage of the S.S. American Star, *Ex-U.S.S.* West Point

Ships being towed to one port or another is a common sight, and certain firms specialize in this type of work. The relatively modern Polish-built seagoing tug and tow ship *Neftegaz 67*, owned by the Ukrainian-based Marman Company, was selected to take the *American*

The S.S. *American Star* ex-U.S.S. *West Point*, ex-S.S. *Australis* ashore on the west coast of Fuerteventura in the Canary Islands. *Steven Tacey*

A beam view of the wreck, which is less than 100 yards from the surf line. *Steven Tacey*

Star from Perama Bay (near Piraeus, Greece) to Thailand. The set speed was 5.5 knots.

In the late evening of December 24, 1993, the *American Star* began her journey behind the *Neftegaz 67,* attached by a stout steel cable. Heavy weather was not anticipated and four port calls were planned. Within 24 hours, the tow captain informed the owners that severe weather was causing the ship to yaw badly. Fearing even greater difficulties as the tow got farther away from land, the *Neftegaz 67* and her charge were ordered back to Piraeus Roads.

A frontal view of the hulk as it sits off a local military reservation. Patrolling soldiers discourage photographers. *Steven Tacey*

A close-up of the bow section and stern half, which has been torn loose and is nearly at a 90-degree angle with the rest of the ship. The stern will soon be gone. *Steven Tacey*

A port-side view of the ship grounded and in the surf line. *Steven Tacey*

Modifications were made on the *American Star*. What amounted to a large sea anchor was fashioned and attached to her stern to alleviate excessive yawing. By December 31, 1993, the tow was again underway.

The drag anchor worked exceptionally well, and two weeks later the tow was proceeding without incident. By January 12, 1993, the tow was out into the Atlantic, having just passed through the Strait of Gibraltar. Unfortunately, the weather again worsened, and by January 15, with high seas and force 12 winds, the main towline was cut and the *American Star* drifted. An attempt was made to secure an emergency towline, but after being made fast, it too was cut to prevent the tow vessel from being dragged under. Not wanting to give up, the *Neftegaz 67* was able to place four specially trained salvage men from its crew onboard the cold hulk. They attempted to tie the tug to the drifting hulk with two polypropylene ropes to at least keep the vessels in close proximity, but this too was unsuccessful. Even the assistance of a Spanish tug, the *Punta Mayor,* was of little value. The bad weather was not abating and soon it became evident

that the sailors aboard the *American Star* would be in peril if not removed. Accordingly, a helicopter evacuated them to Las Palmas, and the drifting ship was on her own.

The *American Star* finally drifted ashore on the west coast of Fuerteventura in the Canary Islands on the morning of January 18, 1994. Within 48 hours, the once proud ship that had transported hundreds of thousands of passengers in peacetime and troops in wartime had broken in two and begun to disintegrate. Today, she continues to show the ravages of time and the elements. Only her forward half is now visible, and the interior of the ship has been gutted by the local populace. All wood fixtures and planking have been removed because the Canary Islands have a very minute supply of lumber. Many visitors photograph the forlorn shipwreck and one German tourist was accidentally killed when he attempted to board the hulk. Now, photographs are forbidden as the wreck site is within a military reservation, and local soldiers chase away the curious. Today all that remains is a rusted bow section of the once proud flagship of the United States Lines and the U.S. Navy transport service.

CHAPTER TWO

EXPLOSION

U.S.S. *Iowa* BB-61
Explosion in Turret 2

U.S.S. Iowa—*Finest Battleship Class of the Twentieth Century*

Without a doubt the *Iowa* class represents the finest class of battleship built in the twentieth century. The four ships of this class, U.S.S. *Iowa* BB-61, U.S.S. *New Jersey* BB-62, U.S.S. *Missouri* BB-63, and U.S.S. *Wisconsin* BB-64, have been prominent in U.S. and world history since May 1938 when the U.S. Navy adopted the design for a new fast battleship. There were to have been two more ships in the class, the U.S.S. *Illinois* BB-65 and U.S.S. *Kentucky* BB-66; however, these ships were dismantled prior to completion and scrapped. The end of World War II signaled the end of battleship construction. A successor design to the *Iowa*'s, the *Montana* (BB-67) class was to have mounted 12 16-inch guns, but the end of World War II caused this class to be stillborn. Thus the *Iowa* class was the last built for the U.S. Navy.

The new battleship U.S.S. *Iowa* BB-61 shortly after being commissioned. She is painted in a dazzle pattern and carries two Kingfisher spotting planes on her stern. The planes were later replaced with helicopters, and her massive close-in antiaircraft batteries were reduced substantially after World War II. *TIM*

A close-up photo of turrets 1 and 2 just after the end of World War II as the U.S.S. *Iowa* leaves San Francisco Bay. *TIM*

Ironically, the *Iowa* design had its roots in the Naval Arms Limitation Treaties first initiated in Washington in 1922. This treaty bound the surviving post-World War I powers to strict limitations in building new ships, namely their tonnage and armament. The original treaty was followed up in 1930 and again in 1936. However, by the early 1930s it became obvious that the treaties had become obsolete tributes to post-World War I resolutions to prevent future war. The world was again on a war footing, and the treaties had little or no force or effect on naval construction.

By 1936, it was apparent that Japan was no longer a party to the naval arms treaties that had attempted to restrict the number and size of various warships, especially the battleship. Japan failed to sign the 1936 accord and with good reason: the Imperial Navy was entertaining the concept of a super battleship—the 69,900-ton, full-load, 27-knot, nine 18-inch gun main battery *Yamato* class. The *Yamato* and sister *Musashi* were laid down in 1937 and 1938, respectively, and although construction was done in utmost secrecy, the international naval community knew of their existence from the day the keel plates swung into place. On the other side of the world, Nazi Germany was building the 52,000-ton *Bismarck* and *Tirpitz* super battleships.

The U.S. Navy, now unhampered by the limits of the international treaties, began to flex its design muscles and the result was the *Iowa* class. The treaty-bound *North Carolina* and *South Dakota*-class battleships, predecessors to the *Iowa's* class, had a main battery of three triple-barrel 16-inch/45-caliber guns, displaced 45,000 tons full load, and had a maximum speed of 28 knots. These highly capable ships conformed to the outer limits of the treaties. They were also considered slow by World War II standards. Clearly a faster, better-armored capital ship was needed to confront the German *Bismarck* (29 knots, eight 15-inch gun main battery) and the Japanese *Yamato* classes. The *Iowa* class combined the best of all characteristics and became the most powerful battleship class in history. This class

The forward 16-inch guns of the *Iowa* pound North Korean targets in May 1952. The shells hit targets 17 miles inland.
TIM - SFCB

was known as the "fast battleship" and was designed to steam at over 32 knots, or fast enough to accompany the attack aircraft carriers into battle.

The new battleships mounted three turrets with triple barrel 16-inch/50-caliber guns that could fire a 2,700-pound projectile up to 42,345 yards. The secondary battery consisted of twenty 5-inch/38-caliber dual purpose guns that could be used against ships or aircraft. Antiaircraft protection initially consisted of a large number of 1.1-inch and 50-caliber machine guns and, based on wartime experience, this was changed to 80 40-millimeter and 49 20-millimeter AA guns. Armor protection was a maximum of 13.5 inches on the hull belt, 17 to 19 inches on the turrets and 17 inches on the conning tower. Speed was in excess of 32 knots and the electronics (radar, fire control) were state-of-the-art. They displaced 57,540 tons full load and carried a wartime crew of over 1,900 men. These were magnificent ships and although the day of the battleship's preeminence in the world's navies

had passed, the *Iowa* class was not looked upon with anything but respect and admiration.

All four of the *Iowa*-class battleships were commissioned during World War II and saw service in the Atlantic and Pacific theaters of combat. Most notably, the U.S.S. *Missouri* hosted the surrender ceremonies of the Japanese Empire in 1945, yet all four ships made a vital contribution to the successful conclusion of the war.

U.S.S. Iowa: *Operational History*

The U.S.S. *Iowa* was launched on August 27, 1942, from her builder's yard at the New York Shipbuilding Company (the slip where she was built had to be enlarged to handle a ship of this size). From the keel laying to the launch, the building process took over two years of hard labor from thousands of skilled shipbuilders. On February 22, 1943, the *Iowa* was commissioned and put to sea. Like her future sister ship the *Missouri*, the *Iowa* touched ground and did some minor damage to her hull while entering Casco Bay, Maine, on July 16, 1943. In November 1943, the new battleship became a target for a torpedo accidentally launched from the escorting destroyer U.S.S. *William D. Porter* DD-579. The battleship was unharmed as were her passengers, which included President Franklin D. Roosevelt.

From her operations in the Atlantic and Mediterranean, the *Iowa* proceeded to the Pacific where she provided shore bombardment and fast carrier protection until war's end. She was then decommissioned and placed in reserve in 1949, only to be brought back in 1951 for service in the Korean War. She bombarded Communist targets and, after the truce was signed, continued in service until 1958, when she again was mothballed.

In the early 1980s, the U.S. Navy was allowed to begin reactivation of the four *Iowa*-class battleships for service with the fleet either as members of carrier battle groups or battleship battle groups. For years, the Navy Department and the U.S. Congress argued as to the viability of the battleship. The aircraft carrier and now the nuclear ballistic missile submarine had surely eclipsed the value of the battleship in the modern technological Navy, or had they? In 1981, reactivation proposals were initiated and slowly all four ships were modernized and equipped with four Phalanx 20-millimeter CIWS (close-in weapons sys-

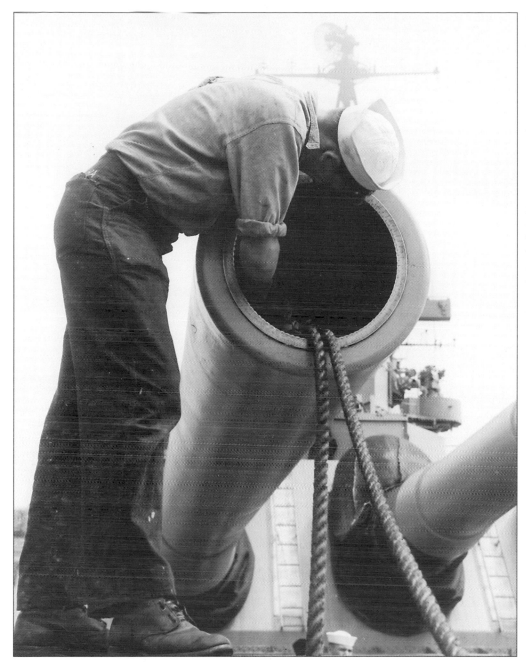

Cleaning the bore of one of the 16-inch guns aboard an *Iowa*-class battleship. The rifled lining is plainly seen. When the flare back occurred aboard the *Iowa*, the 1,900-pound shell was flung 44 inches into the barrel of the gun—which demonstrated the power of an open breech explosion. *TIM - SFCB*

tems), 32 Tomahawk cruise missile launchers, and 16 Harpoon antiship missile launchers.

Electronic capability was upgraded and now the U.S. Marines had a heavy-gun, shore-bombardment support weapon in the 16-inch and 5-inch guns, and the Navy had fast ships capable of firing the most modern missiles, yet able to survive even the most horrendous Soviet missile attacks. Although these ships were ancient by any standard, they were still the most powerful in the world.

After being modernized at the Avondale Shipyard in Westwego, Louisiana, the *Iowa*

assumed her role in naval operations. She participated in a number of operations and, most important, developed procedures and practices for accurate, reliable, safe, and fast firing of her main battery. The 16-inch guns were five decades old, and the vast majority of the men who had originally perfected their skill with this weapon were no longer available. It fell to new officers and men to learn an old trade. In 1982, the U.S.S. *New Jersey* had fired a number of rounds in Beirut against Syrian artillery emplacements with dismal results in overall accuracy. There was obviously some

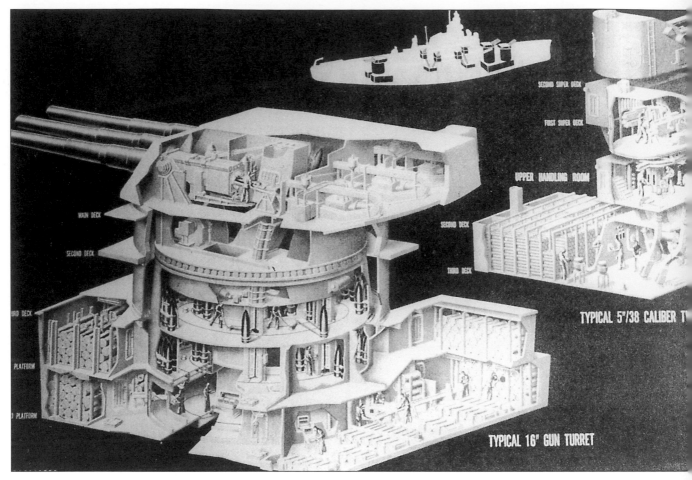

Labels on image: SECOND SUPER DECK, FIRST SUPER DECK, UPPER HANDLING ROOM, SECOND DECK, THIRD DECK, MAIN DECK, SECOND DECK, 3RD DECK, PLATFORM, D PLATFORM, TYPICAL 5"/38 CALIBER T', TYPICAL 16" GUN TURRET

The typical 16-inch gun turret aboard a World War II battleship. The men in the rotating structure of this turret were immediately killed during the April 19, 1989, flare back of the center gun. Eleven men in the lower magazine were saved, thus proving the soundness of the design of this ship. *Author's Collection*

concern about this and other difficulties with the 16-inch gun. The Navy then contracted with RCA to develop a 36- to 42-week course in the operation of this weapon, yet the balance of safety and sensibility with the desire for minimum time between firings was fragile.

April 19, 1989: Turret 2 Explosion Aboard the U.S.S. Iowa

Naval history is rife with various disasters, many unexplained, but it is rare that sabotage or deliberate acts are the causes. Investigators easily can trace most tragedies to human and mechanical error or both. Often, this determination is made only after exhaustive study of forensics, survivor testimony, and intelligent analysis. Unfortunately, the turret explosion aboard the *Iowa* not only cost the lives of 47 men, but further embarrassed the U.S. Navy

when its investigation teams proposed some very lurid scenarios for the reason why.

On the morning of April 19, 1989, the ship was operating in the Caribbean on an exercise dubbed FLEETEX 3-89. This involved the test firing of her main battery with a variety of charges. After turret 1 had fired, turret 2 began its loading and firing sequence upon instructions from the bridge. All three barrels were to be loaded with dummy shells and D846 propellant. A five-bag charge was selected, and although the use of this type of propellant in this environment was unusual, it was not considered unsafe. The maximum pounds per square inch with this charge was in the 39,000 psi range, substantially lower than the normal pressure of 49,700 psi, and well within the 90,000 psi maximum.

Within 44 seconds of the command, barrels one and three were loaded and ready. Barrel two had been loaded with its projectile, and next came powder bags 1 and 2 that would be followed up by three more bags, all rammed in at a slow speed. The turret captain, Senior Chief Gunners Mate Reginald Ziegler, complimented the loading of the left barrel, and then he was heard to say that there was some difficulty with the center barrel. "We'll straighten that out," the bridge promised. Within seconds, Richard Lawrence, center gun cradleman, stated, "I have a problem here; I am not ready yet." Ziegler informed Lt. (jg) Robert Buch, "Tell pilot we are not ready yet. There is a problem in the center gun!"

Not long after this exchange, Lawrence again complained, "I am not ready yet! I am not ready yet!" The next and last voice simply uttered, "Oh my . . ." A huge fireball then swept through the entire turret and erupted through the gun bloomers that were attached to the barrels outside the turret. The flare back consumed the interior of the turret and 47 men were killed outright. The fire did not spread to the magazine; if it had, an explosion only rivaled by that of the H.M.S. *Hood* after being hit by the German battleship *Bismarck* would have vaporized the entire ship. Antiflash seals in the scuttles to the powder magazine saved the ship as well as 11 crewmen down below the rotating turret system.

The heat generated was intense and hot gasses burned the teak deck around the turret. An order to flood the magazine quickly ended any further possibility of explosion, yet it took over 90 minutes to extinguish all of the fires.

What had caused this explosion to occur?

The Navy initiated two major investigations both of which did not discount sabotage or deliberate mishandling of powder in the turret. At one press briefing, Admiral Richard Milligan, who led one of the investigations, stated in September 1989 that Acting Gun Captain Clarence Hartwig was more than likely responsible for the tragedy! The press and many in the public decried these reports as being self-serving and the conclusions absurd. They further charged that the reports served to cover up the obvious—old ammunition, outdated ship technology, and poor training all in the name of saving the battleship from oblivion. The Navy, to its credit, did test as many variables as was reasonably possible, but the findings were initially inconclusive.

The Sandia National Laboratories, in conjunction with the Navy, carried out further analysis. Their findings were more forensic

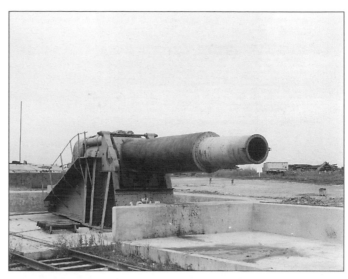

A test gun at the Naval Proving Ground at Dalgren, Virginia. Investigators carried out extensive testing at this facility to determine the cause of the turret explosion aboard the U.S.S. *Iowa*. TIM - SFCB

The number 2 turret as the flare back occurs. Smoke pours out of the apertures around the barrels. *Navy League*

and less humanistic in nature. In essence, the explosive pellets (tubular nitrocellulose) in the trim layer could have been too few in number in this particular bag. If the mechanical bag rammer was set on fast rather than slow speed as required for five bags, then it was possible that a pre-ignition could have taken place before the breech was closed. Extensive testing indicated this as the most prominent cause, and that is the most accepted explanation of the flare back. In any event, 47 lives were lost in one of yet another tragedy of the sea.

A 16-inch shell rams into a gun barrel onboard a modern battleship. *USNI*

The dead are brought home. *Navy League*

Firefighters pour water all over the number 2 turret and surrounding area to prevent an even greater tragedy aboard the *Iowa*. *Navy League*

U.S.S. *Mississippi* BB-41
Two Flare Backs in the Same Barrel— 20 Years Apart

The U.S.S. *Mississippi* BB-41 was one of the three *New Mexico*-class battleships built during World War I. In an appropriation that included other major warships for a growing Navy, the U.S. Congress authorized the construction of the *Mississippi* for no more than $7.8 million, and granted the contract to the Newport News Shipbuilding and Drydock Company. The *Mississippi* was laid down on April 5, 1915; launched on January 25, 1917; and put into commission on December 18, 1917.

New Mexico-Class Battleships

The *New Mexico*-class battleships were powerful and brutish-looking ships that were easily identified by their clipper bow. The three ships of the class, U.S.S. *New Mexico* BB-40, U.S.S. *Mississippi* BB-41, and U.S.S. *Idaho* BB-42, were improved versions of their immediate predecessors, the *Pennsylvania* and *Nevada* classes. In all, the U.S. Navy either built or was building six identifiable battleship classes during the 10-year period from 1911 to 1921.

There would have been a seventh class but for the restrictions of the Washington Naval Arms Limitation Treaty of 1922. The *New Mexico* class was the fourth of the six classes and inaugurated the use of the 14-inch/50-caliber gun in its four-turret, 12-barrel main battery. Each barrel in the triple turret was mounted in a separate sleeve, another departure from past practice. This class also abandoned the casemate guns of the 5-inch secondary battery located in hull apertures and sited four 5-inch/51-caliber guns on the boat deck. Later, open 5-inch/25-caliber dual-purpose mounts replaced the 5-inch/51-caliber guns as the fleet began to slowly recognize the threat of aircraft.

Aside from her main battery, the *Mississippi* mounted 12 5-inch/51-caliber guns either in open sites or in evenly spaced main deck casemates. There were eight 3-inch antiaircraft guns and two submerged torpedo tubes that could fire 21-inch antiship torpedoes from openings in the hull. The torpedo capability was later scrapped as a concept, and air defense became more important as evidenced by the addition of 3-inch guns and 50-caliber machine guns.

She was well armored in an "all-or-nothing" format where only critical areas (maga-

The U.S.S. *Mississippi* BB-41 rides at anchor shortly after being commissioned in December 1917. Like most U.S. battleships built during and shortly after World War I, cage masts and heavy radio antennas dominate the upper works. *TIM*

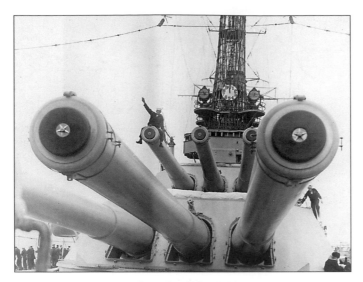

Gun barrels of the *Mississippi*'s two forward turrets. The center barrel of the upper turret experienced the flare back. A range-finder clock is attached to the cage mast above the navigating bridge. *TIM*

zines, conning tower, and engine spaces) were heavily protected with built-in armored steel. The main battery turrets were protected with 9-inch to 18-inch plating as were the shell-handling areas. All other ship's compartments were protected against shell fragments and small-arms fire with lighter shell plating.

The *Mississippi* displaced 33,000 tons full load and was 624 feet in length. Her beam was 97.5 feet and her draught was 31 feet. As there was no requirement yet for the "fast" battleship, her speed was 21 knots, and only slightly higher if the hull was clean and the maximum 32,000 horsepower was on line. She was driven by Curtis four shaft-geared (cruising) turbines turning four screws. Power came from nine Babcock and Wilcox boilers and she carried 2,200 tons of naval fuel oil.

The *New Mexico*-class battleships were well-founded and stable platforms for their 14-inch main battery. All three ships proved their worth during World War II, providing artillery support for amphibious operations and other land assault operations.

U.S.S. Mississippi—
Operational History

The *Mississippi* went to sea as a fleet unit in December 1917, and began a series of training exercises in the Caribbean area. For the balance of World War I, which ended on

The *Mississippi* has just fired her main battery during target practice off the southern California coast. All guns are turned to starboard for a 12-gun salvo of 1,500-pound target shells. *TIM*

November 11, 1918, the new battleship remained in home waters. The *Mississippi* and other modern oil-burning U.S. battleships did not join with the Royal Navy to operate against the Imperial German Navy because of fuel availability. Even though the United States had entered the war against Germany, there was little oil to spare in England. Consequently only those U.S. battleships that burned coal were assigned to the war zone.

In mid-1919, the *Mississippi* (now nick-named the "Missy") was transferred to the Pacific and home-ported in San Pedro Bay. There she remained until 1940 when she was transferred back to the Atlantic Fleet. Sister battleships *New Mexico* and *Idaho* were also home ported in San Pedro along with 10 other battleships on a rotational basis. It was from the San Pedro Bay anchorage that the *Mississippi* steamed out in company with other capital ships, including the U.S.S. *Tennessee* BB-43, for what was announced as secret gunnery practice off the southern California coast. Gunnery exercises were to begin on June 12, 1924, for selected battleship divisions.

Turret Explosion— Center Barrel, Turret 2 (June 12, 1924)

The *Mississippi* was carrying a number of gunnery experts and observers from sister ship *New Mexico* to watch and meter the behavior of the 14-inch/50-caliber main battery. This weapon was carried on 5 of the 15 active inter-war battleships and initially it was considered far more effective than the 14-inch/45-caliber guns of the *Pennsylvania* and *Nevada* classes. Unfortunately, the gun was plagued with a number of problems ranging from misses at long range to shells not properly seated when the barrels were elevated to maximum height. It was to be further tested off San Pedro.

The triple-barrel turret of the *Mississippi* was able to fire one salvo per minute based on loading time limitations. The loading angle required that the barrel be trained to zero degrees, thus after each firing the gun was returned to its original position. The three barrels of the turret were fed by two shell hoists that, due to their location, slightly disadvantaged the center gun in terms of shell handling. The target shells weighed 1,500 pounds and the muzzle velocity was 1,935 feet per second. Four propellant or powder charges weighed 470 pounds. The charge was finely

A view of the memorial ceremony for the men killed in turret 2 on June 12, 1924. Over 25,000 attended. *Author's Collection*

The breech of a large-caliber weapon in a battleship. This area must be clear of flaming debris before the next shoot. The breech is closed mechanically and screwed down to prevent a back blast. *Author's Collection*

The *Mississippi* fires her secondary battery as smoke and gas engulf turret 2. Water used in fire fighting is being discharged over the side adjacent to the turret. This photo was taken by a nearby ship just after the flare back on November 20, 1943. *Author's Collection*

sewn into cylindrical silk bags that would be consumed during the explosion and hopefully leave no burning residue. Powder charges were hoisted to each barrel separately and hand-fed onto a loading tray. Like the shell that came before, the charges were mechanically rammed into the barrel. The breech was closed and locked. The gun was then ready to fire.

A typical turret had a crew of over 45 men and, in the case of turret 2 aboard the *Mississippi,* the crew consisted of 3 officers and 45 men. As the eighth salvo was being prepared, a problem was discovered with the loading of barrel number two, and before the breech could be closed, the four powder bags ignited and a flare back engulfed the turret. Powder bags in the upper handling room that were about to be brought up for loading were also consumed and the entire upper turret structure was subjected to intense flame and poisonous gasses. Forty-eight men died almost instantly and many others were overcome by fumes and noxious clouds of gas from the smoldering turret.

Within moments, the order came down to flood the magazine and secure all doors to prevent fire from spreading. When fire-fighting crews found their way into the turret, they discovered that little had actually burned. The flare back destroyed electric servo motors and

After the fire and rescue crew secured the area, they lifted men down from the exit port under turret 2. *Author's Collection*

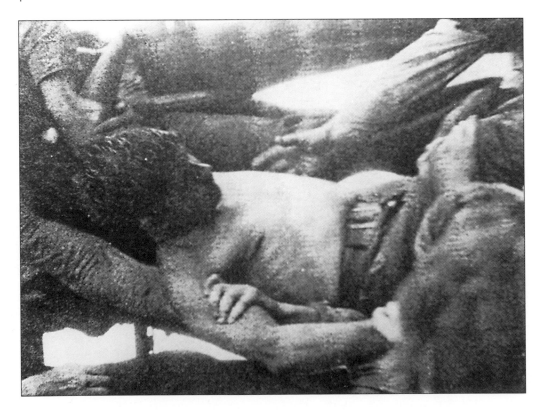

burned other readily flammable items, but it did not harm the turret and guns. The *Mississippi* was ordered to proceed to San Pedro for temporary repairs and have the dead and injured taken ashore. A memorial that included over 25,000 mourners was held in San Pedro on June 17, 1924.

An inquiry into the cause of this accident was initiated, and like those convened to investigate the turret explosions on the heavy cruiser U.S.S. *St. Paul* CA-73 (April 21, 1952), the battleship U.S.S. *Iowa* BB-61 (April 19, 1989), and oddly again on the *Mississippi* (November 20, 1944), there was only informed speculation. The nature of a flare back is that it completely destroys everything flammable in its path and kills all human observers who might be able to shed some light on the reason or reasons for the explosion. The strength of a capital ship turret and its surrounding structure confine the effects of a flare back, and should the conflagration spread to the magazine, an explosion similar to that on the U.S.S. *Arizona* on December 7, 1941, could occur.

The center barrel had been loaded with its target shell and four bags rammed home; however, the gun captain was unable to mechanically shut and lock the breech before the flare back. A lone surviving observer noticed that the gun captain appeared to have seen a small flash in the barrel and was attempting to manually close the breech as quickly as possible. This led the investigators to conclude that a fire or burning particles from a prior shoot had remained in the powder bag seating area of the barrel. This in turn ignited the silk bag or bags.

Spent or smoldering particles that might be present in the barrel are expelled by a 140-pound air pressure blast that is designed to cleanse the barrel and make it safe for the next shoot. The center barrel only registered 110 pounds. In essence, there likely was some burning residue in the barrel that ignited the next charge and caused the flare back before the gun captain could shut the breech.

To add injury to insult, shortly after the *Mississippi* anchored in San Pedro Bay, the port barrel in turret 2 discharged. The swaying hand of one of the dead who was being evacuated from the turret accidentally activated the firing switch. No further damage was done to the ship and the shell landed harmlessly in the sea.

Turret 2 Explosion—
Center Barrel (November 20, 1943)

The *Mississippi* served in World War II primarily as a convoy escort and shore bombardment platform. It was in the latter role that an accident almost identical to that which had occurred nearly two decades before occurred off the Japanese-held island of Makin.

Early on November 20, 1943, a shore bombardment of Makin Island in the Gilbert Islands began with the *Mississippi* and other heavy units selectively hitting enemy positions with main and secondary battery fire. Just as the first wave of the assault force was on its way to the beach, all ships went to rapid fire to disrupt and confuse Japanese defenders. *Mississippi* gunners were firing all guns as fast as they could be loaded, and suddenly gas and smoke erupted from the range finder ports on either side of turret 2. The bridge telephone talker was asked to contact the turret. There was no answer. Incredibly, there had been a repeat of the June 1924 tragedy; 42 men and 1 officer were dead. Powder bags being loaded into the center gun had ignited, probably from smoldering debris left over during the haste of continuous firing. From there, other powder charges had burned in the upper handling room. In addition to the dead, 19 men were injured, and the same damage was done to the turret as that in 1924. In 1944, however, the ship did not leave the line for repairs—she kept on firing to support the landing force. As in 1924, all witnesses who might have pinpointed the cause were lost. A memorial was held shortly after Makin was secured.

Epilogue

For identical accidents to occur 20 years apart in the same turret, especially in view of turret redesign and safety training, is a mystery to this day. In the first instance, a faulty air injector was likely at fault; in the second, probably a certain degree of carelessness due to the heat of battle. A total of 91 men were lost.

The U.S.S. *Mississippi* went on to serve the Navy as a test platform for missiles and other post-World War II naval weapons. She ended her career as AG-128 (auxiliary) and was sold for scrap in November 1956. Of the 15 interwar battleships, the *Mississippi* endured for the longest period—39 years. The turret explosions have never really been explained and went down in history as two of the worst naval tragedies in the twentieth century.

The *Mississippi* in her final configuration. No longer a battleship, she is used for evaluating surface-to-air missiles and other naval weapons in the immediate post-World War II era. She carries 5-inch, 6-inch, and 3-inch guns as well as guided missiles—only for testing. *Author's Collection*

The 39-year-old *Mississippi* quietly awaits her turn to be scrapped in December 1956. *TIM - SFCB*

U.S.S. *Turner* DD-648
Lost without Warning

On January 3, 1944, the U.S.S. *Turner* DD-648 suffered explosions originating near her bow that continued along her 348-foot length until the new destroyer literally was annihilated. She eventually sank and 138 of her crew were killed in the two-hour ordeal. It was not a loss through combat as she was anchored in protected waters off the Ambrose Light near New York Harbor. This was a human error involving one of wartime's more unstable antisubmarine weapons—the Mousetrap.

U.S.S. Turner:
A Gleaves-Class Destroyer

The U.S.S. *Turner* DD-648 was a World War II built destroyer that displaced 1,630 tons (2,000 tons full load) and was 348 feet 4 inches in length with a beam that was 36 feet 1 inch. She developed 50,200 horsepower from her two steam-geared turbines and had a designed speed of 35 knots. She was originally designed as a *Gleaves*-class destroyer, yet more closely resembled a subcategory designated after the lead ship, the U.S.S. *Bristol* DD-453. She was one of a large number of assembly-line-constructed destroyers based on pre-World War II planning, and was the predecessor class to the highly popular *Fletcher*'s. What distinguished the *Turner* from the *Gleaves* class was the absence of the number three 5-inch/38-caliber mount and one of the five tube torpedo batteries. It had been decided a year before the war that a certain number of *Gleaves*-class destroyers would be modified for more intensive antiaircraft capability as well as improved antisubmarine warfare platforms. Accordingly, the *Turner* was armed with four rather than five 5-inch/38-caliber guns, and dispensed with a five-tube bank of 21-inch antiship torpedoes. She was then re-armed with a 1.1-inch AA gun aft and a much improved depth charge capability to meet the anticipated needs of the unfolding Atlantic war. Ultimately, the cranky 1.1-inch AA gun was to be replaced with two twin 40-millimeter *bofors* guns, but there was great demand for these weapons in the fleet so installation

February 28, 1943, launching day for the brand-new *Bristol*-class destroyer, U.S.S. *Turner* DD-648. Her cost of $8.8 million is small compared to the 1990s *Arleigh Burke*-class destroyer that cost approximately $1 billion. *TIM - SFCB*

A quarter view of the *Turner* as she was moored in New York. The Mousetrap ASW weapon has not yet been fitted. *TIM - SFCB*

aboard the *Turner* was delayed. However, a number of 20-millimeter close-in defense guns were installed in selected locations.

The Federal Shipbuilding and Drydock Company built the *Turner* in Kearny, New Jersey, and launched her on February 28, 1943. A month and a half later, on April 15, 1943, the new destroyer was commissioned and began her working-up period. She carried a wartime complement of 261 officers and men and, under the command of Lt. Commander Henry S. Wygant, left for Casco, Maine. Here she began a series of exercises to prepare her crew for modern antisubmarine warfare. For the next four months, the *Turner* acted as an escort for convoys transiting the Atlantic to various new Allied ports. Her first real action with the enemy occurred on the night of October 23, 1943, as she was escorting a westbound convoy to the United States. The convoy, designated GUS-18, was comprised of 66 merchant ships, 8 destroyers, a minesweeper, and the U.S.C.G.C. *Spencer*. The convoy picked up ships all over the Mediterranean and ultimately began its Atlantic crossing at a set speed of 8 knots. The ships would split up for either New

York or Norfolk when close to the eastern seaboard of the United States.

The *Turner* was stationed in the point position 7.5 miles in front of the main body and at approximately 7:30 P.M., her surface radar (SG) detected a surfaced object off her port quarter. After 11 minutes of radar tracking, the excited lookouts shouted that there was an enemy submarine running on the surface 500 yards off the port quarter. In a series of actions played out on many destroyer bridges in World War II in all navies, the captain ordered full ahead and every gun that would bear to open fire and keep firing. The *Turner* charged down on the submarine as the Germans frantically attempted to submerge. Finally the U-boat began its dive. Just as the hunter approached, the submarine disappeared, but not before she had been showered with 20-millimeter, 40-millimeter, and 5-inch gunfire, which included a direct hit by the main battery. Passing over the spot where the submarine dived, the *Turner* fired two charges from her port K-gun followed up by a single charge from her stern rack of depth charges. Moments later a huge underwater explosion was felt, and within minutes eyewitnesses watched an object resembling a submarine broach the surface,

The Mousetrap rail with four rocket-propelled depth bombs. This particular Mousetrap was aboard a smaller vessel. The Hedgehog proved too heavy for most smaller patrol ships, thus the Mousetrap was installed. *Author's Collection*

Lucky survivors of the *Turner*'s loss in January 1944. Nearly half of the crew of 299 were killed as the ship exploded, including her commanding officer, Lt. Commander Wygant. *TIM - SFCB*

A young sailor utters a silent prayer for his departed shipmates during breakfast shortly after the survivors were brought in to a local naval station. *TIM - SFCB*

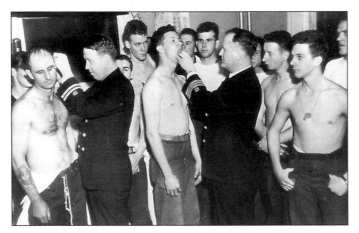

Navy physicians examine survivors of the *Turner* after the wounded came ashore on January 3, 1944. Sixty of the 161 survivors were injured and many were hospitalized for weeks or months. *TIM - SFCB*

upend to a 70-degree angle, and sink. Despite this evidence, 10th Fleet staff refused to give credit for a kill. The *Turner* continued with the convoy without incident and, shortly after returning to the United States in November 1943, had a new type of antisubmarine warfare weapon installed—the Mousetrap projectile launcher.

The Mousetrap:
A New Antisubmarine Weapon

The Mousetrap consisted of a series of pattern-aimed rails that contained eight forward-thrown, 65-pound, rocket-propelled depth bombs. The rails were splayed to allow rockets to land in a certain preset pattern. The advantage of this Royal Navy-designed weapon was that it could be fired in front of the ship, thus allowing continued sound contact with the target. Its downside was that the torpex-filled projectile was not sufficiently powerful to kill a submerged submarine, but in theory could damage it sufficiently to cause it to surface and defend itself with its deck guns.

The three "8 bomb traps" were affixed to its host destroyer just forward of the number one 5-inch mount and when fired would fan out to form a circular pattern far ahead of the ship. A serious limitation of the Mousetrap was that it was not trainable, and there was no method of compensating for the ship's roll. Due to their sensitivity, the depth bombs exploded upon contact with a submerged submarine or other object. Doctrine held that an initial attack could be followed up by a more

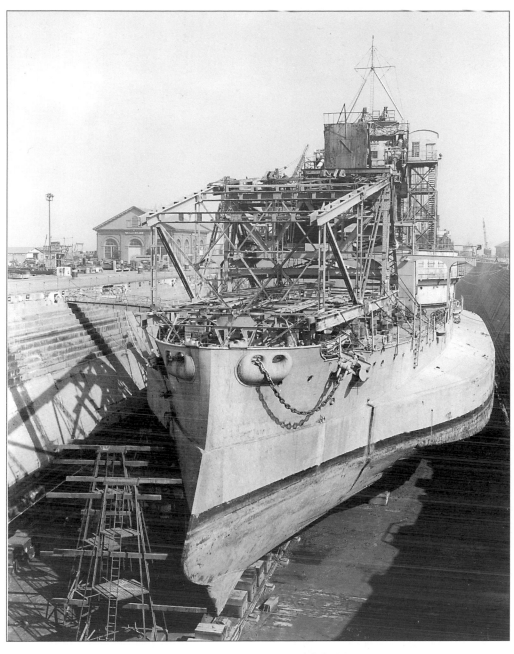

The U.S.S. *Craneship* AB-1 (formerly the battleship U.S.S. *Kearsarge*) in dry dock. The old pre-World War I battleship was equipped with a heavy-capacity crane and large external bulges for stability. The ungainly ship was perfect for salvage work. *Author's Collection*

conventional concentrated depth charge attack for maximum effectiveness. The Mousetrap was preferable to the other alternative, the Hedgehog. The Hedgehog's spigot launcher was heavy; when fired, the weapon caused a massive recoil that was unacceptable in the smaller antisubmarine ships. However, on the plus side, it was a simple weapon with a far greater range.

The Mousetrap was installed on *Benson–Livermore* (*Gleaves*)-class destroyers, and by the beginning of 1944, 12 destroyer-type ships were actively capable of using this weapon.

Loss of the Turner:
January 3, 1944

The *Turner* returned to U.S. home waters on January 1, 1944, having been part of a Task Force 64 on routine convoy escort. The eastbound convoy split into two groups, one for New York and the other for Norfolk. The *Turner* accompanied the New York group and anchored off the Ambrose Light on the evening of January 2. Understandably, the crew was anxious for stateside liberty and many had what was commonly termed "channel fever"—so close yet so far. The sleek destroyer swung at anchor for several hours

The U.S.S. *Craneship* hoists the bow of the *Turner* out of the water. Just as the structure surfaced, the chains used to lift it broke and the twisted metal slipped back into the channel. A decision was made to remove everything else possible, and then have divers cut up the remains and bring pieces up for scrap. *TIM - SFCB*

awaiting sunrise and permission to enter the harbor. One of the precautions required of armed naval vessels was that all weapons be disarmed, and ammunition either stored properly or off-loaded for safety.

Early in the morning watch, a gunners mate was attempting to place the Mousetrap rocket-propelled depth bombs on safety prior to entering the inner harbor. During this procedure, at or about 6:18 A.M., the forward part of the ship erupted in a series of explosions that brightened the early morning. The explosions continued in their intensity, killing some of the crew who were in the crew's mess and berthing quarters just beneath or in close proximity to the Mousetraps above. The carnage was not restricted to the forward end of the ship as smoke and deadly fumes were forced into many of the ship's compartments. Aside from the death and destruction below, dead, dying, and wounded men who had been subjected to flying steel and concussion covered the decks. Out of a sheer desire to survive, men began to retreat to the aft part of the ship. The injured huddled on the fantail of the

now listing destroyer as others up forward attempted to bring fire hoses into play. It was too late.

It was only a matter of time before the forward 5-inch handling rooms and magazines were engulfed in explosions and the stored ammunition went up. The number two 5-inch mount was blown loose from its location on the superstructure and disappeared in the smoke. The number one 5-inch turret was simply a twisted mass of steel. Secondary explosions from stored ammunition forcibly tore the ship in half and destroyed the forward areas. As the explosions continued, all but two of the ship's officers were killed and radio communication was rendered impossible when the mast and radio antennas were destroyed. Fortunately, nearby ships witnessed the first detonations and began to come to the stricken destroyer's aid. Anchored just under 2 miles distant, the destroyer escort U.S.S. *Swasey* DE-248 was underway within minutes of hearing the first explosions and by 6:45 A.M. was within 500 yards of the burning ship. She launched a whaleboat with a fire and res-

A Coast Guard *Sikorsky HNS-1* helicopter like the one used to bring medical supplies to the injured crew from the *Turner*. *Author's Collection*

their shipmates, the efforts of the rescuers, and blood plasma flown by helicopter from New York to Sandy Hook. This was the inaugural use of the brand-new *USCG Sikorsky HNS-1* helicopter piloted by Coast Guard Lt. Commander Frank Erickson.

The loss of the *Turner* was generally attributed to the improper handling of one or more of the rocket-propelled Mousetrap depth bombs, one of which presumably detonated. This triggered a series of secondary explosions that progressively consumed the ship from bow to stern. This was not to be the first instance of the Mousetrap being suspected of lethal damage to its host ship. On April 30, 1946, the destroyer escort U.S.S. *Solar* DE-221, along with much of the nearby pier, was destroyed when off-loading ammunition. The highly sensitive Mousetrap explosive was again cited for the incident. Long before this, however, the Mousetrap had been removed from all of the destroyers and was eventually deleted as an ASW weapon.

The ill-fated *Turner* sank in 60 feet of water in a well-traveled shipping lane. It was imperative that her hulk be raised or demolished. The U.S.S. *Craneship* AB-1 was dispatched in mid-1944 to remove the wreck's major subsurface portions. In 1948, much of the remaining hulk was further blasted down to a lower level. In spite of this, a very deep draft supertanker, the *Aeolis*, struck an isolated projection from the *Turner* and also became a victim in 1976. The *Aeolis* was later refloated and since that time no further incidents have occurred. The remainder of the once proud destroyer now lies quietly unmolested in the sand off New York.

cue team, and then proceeded to come along side the burning destroyer to ply her fire hoses on one of the many fires.

Many of the *Turner's* crew now found themselves in the water, where Coast Guard boats and the whaleboat from the *Swasey* rescued them. The inferno aboard the *Turner*, however, had now reached beyond the forward superstructure and was consuming the entire ship. By this time, Coast Guard cutters and other rescue boats were pulling men off the stern, and at 7:50 A.M., there was another massive explosion. It occurred just aft of the number two stack, probably in the engine room, and combined with the 5-inch magazine literally devastated what was left of the dying destroyer.

The *Turner* capsized to starboard and slowly sank. Most of her twisted remains finally disappeared in 60 feet of water at 8:27 A.M.

Epilogue

The explosions that rocked the *Turner* sank her after over two hours of agony and resulted in the death of 15 of her 17 officers (2 junior ensigns survived) and 123 enlisted men; 161 men survived. Of the survivors, 60 were injured and required extensive hospitalization. Many owe their lives to the bravery of

The destroyer escort U.S.S *Swasey* DE-248, which remained alongside the dying destroyer and rendered assistance in spite of the danger. *USNI and U.S. Navy*

FIRE

U.S.S. *Enterprise* CVAN-65
Fire Aboard the Largest Warship in the World

During the late 1960s, the U.S. Navy was plagued with three major fires aboard its attack carriers. The first was the U.S.S. *Oriskany* CVA-34 on October 26, 1966; the second on the U.S.S. *Forrestal* CVA-59 on July 29, 1967; and finally, on January 14, 1969, on the U.S.S. *Enterprise* CVAN-65, the world's first nuclear carrier. On the "Big E" 28 crewmen lost their lives, and 344 others were injured (65 seriously); the ship was severely damaged and 15 aircraft were destroyed.

Building on past experience, the Navy had developed safety procedures and fire-fighting techniques specifically designed to prevent such a disaster. However, in the activity always present on the flight deck of a supercarrier, there is always the chance of an accident, especially when heavy

The nuclear aircraft carrier U.S.S. *Enterprise* CVAN-65 enters Pearl Harbor with her crew lining the side in a demonstration of respect for the U.S.S. *Arizona* Memorial. The destroyer U.S.S. *Morton* DD-948 is moored in the left background. *TIM*

ordnance is being loaded. On January 14, 1969, the deck of the *Enterprise* was crowded with bomb- and rocket-laden aircraft awaiting the launch signal when disaster struck.

U.S.S. Enterprise *CVAN-65: The First Nuclear-Powered Surface Ship*

The U.S. Navy began building nuclear-powered submarines in the early 1950s, and it was not long before the surface Navy wanted nuclear-powered ships of their own. An aircraft carrier was the likely candidate and on August 16, 1957, the Newport News Shipbuilding and Drydock Company was selected to build what would be the largest warship in history. The contract was for $450 million. Three years later, on September 24, 1960, the U.S.S. *Enterprise*, the eighth ship in the U.S. Navy to bear that name, was launched. Building this ship presented a number of difficulties to the yard, yet builders overcame them and on November 25, 1961, she was commissioned.

Her overall design length was 1,102 feet with a maximum flight deck width of 252 feet. The full load displacement was 89,600 tons and she attained speeds in excess of 35 knots during sea trials. Eight A2W nuclear reactors (developed by a joint venture of the Navy and the Atomic Energy Commission) powered the new carrier. The reactors generated over 280,000 shaft horsepower, but the value of nuclear power was most evident in the ship's independence from conventional fueling. The *Enterprise* steamed 207,000 miles on her original uranium cores. By 1994, the duration of her fuel cores had improved fourfold. Nuclear power renders the supercarrier available at almost a moment's notice. The nuclear super carriers are rightfully described by the Navy as, "4.5 acres of U.S. sovereignty anywhere on the world's oceans."

Aside from range and speed, the *Enterprise* depends on her heavily armored flight deck for protection. The value of an armored flight deck has been proven time and time again, but most graphically on January 14, 1969, when the carrier was ravaged by nine major-caliber bombs and intense fires.

When first introduced to the fleet, the Big E had a turban-topped island that mounted the Hughes-fixed array radar system that provided a constant 360-degree, three-dimensional view. The new carrier was also equipped

An ordnance technician checks a Zuni high-velocity aircraft rocket pod. The Zuni was capable of 1,400 knots and weighed 150 pounds. This type of rocket accidentally ignited on the *Enterprise* and U.S.S. *Forrestal* CVA-59 and the results were tragic for both carriers. *Author's Collection*

with the NTDS (Naval Tactical Data System), which allows its host to automatically track and monitor a number of diverse targets and potential threats. Taken together, these two systems were the immediate precursors to AEGIS, the present-day electronic tracking and umbrella defense system operational in many combat ships of the 1990s.

Her armament consists of 85 to 95 aircraft of all types and capability, and for ship defense there is the Sea Sparrow point defense missiles and Vulcan Phalanx 20-millimeter CIWS. Her crew of 5,695 personnel consists of 3,215 ship's company and 2,480 in the air wing.

Fleet Duty

After a period of familiarization for the crew on this revolutionary ship, she was deployed to the Mediterranean where the Soviet Navy watched her closely. (In "one-upmanship," the U.S. Navy had surged ahead of its fellow superpower.) In October 1962, the *Enterprise* diverted from her home port of Norfolk, Virginia, and entered the Caribbean in preparation for world war. The Cuban Missile Crisis brought the superpowers to the verge of World War III, and if necessary, the *Enterprise* would launch against Soviet and Cuban targets. However, the "quarantine," or naval blockade, of Cuba caused the Soviet government to reconsider, and by December 1962 the crisis had passed.

Explosion and fire wrack the aft flight deck of the *Enterprise* on the morning of January 14, 1969. Firefighters attempt to bring the blazing inferno under control, but it takes 41 minutes. *USNI*

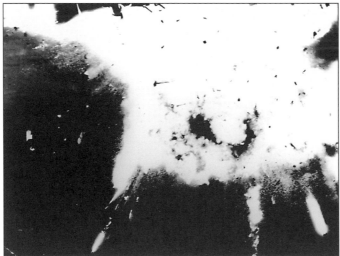

A bomb detonates on the flight deck of the *Enterprise*. *USNI*

In the summer of 1964, "power projection" was demonstrated to the world by *Operation Sea Orbit*. Nuclear-powered escorts U.S.S. *Long Beach* CGN-9 and U.S.S. *Bainbridge* DLGN-25 accompanied the *Enterprise* on an around-the-world cruise. This cruise was notable in that the 30,565-mile voyage was entirely self-reliant. At no time did these ships reprovision from any shore station. This proved the value of nuclear energy as a source of power for the surface Navy, at least from a geopolitical standpoint. However, taxpayer cost quietly put an end to the concept of an all-nuclear Navy. Only aircraft carriers and submarines have been and continue to be candidates for nuclear power. The Navy never repeated prototypes *Long Beach* and *Bainbridge*, and in the early 1990s the Navy decommissioned them.

Just as *Operation Sea Orbit* was ending, war in Southeast Asia was beginning in earnest. The Vietnamese civil war had escalated and the United States was progressively drawn in as a major participant. The *Enterprise* made a number of deployments into the Western Pacific after her refueling in October 1964. Her aircraft destroyed targets all over Vietnam and provided support to ground forces from either Dixie Station or Yankee Station off the coast.

She was on station and prepared to launch against North Korea in January 1968 after their navy seized the intelligence-gathering ship U.S.S. *Pueblo* AGER-2. No action was taken, and the crew was set free a year later after prolonged negotiation.

In the fall of 1968, the *Enterprise* entered the Puget Sound Naval Shipyard in Bremerton, Washington, for a brief overhaul. The Big E returned to the Alameda Naval Air Station and after a period of working up, left San Francisco for the Hawaiian Islands on January 6, 1969. The carrier was scheduled for air operations and bombing practice at Kahoolawe Island in mid-January 1969.

Disaster on the Flight Deck

Early on the morning of January 14, 1969, the *Enterprise* was operating 70 miles southwest of Pearl Harbor and had just launched 15 aircraft for practice bombing and strafing runs on the target range at nearby Kahoolawe Island. A subsequent flight of 30

The U.S.S. *Rogers* DD-186 steams close aboard and plies all of her fire hoses on the deck of the burning carrier. *Navy League*

aircraft including F-4 Phantoms fighters and A-6 Intruder attack bombers was being equipped for a similar exercise with takeoff scheduled at 8:30 A.M. The 30-aircraft practice strike would take less than 8 minutes to launch as the *Enterprise* could catapult them at intervals of 15 seconds each.

Fifteen minutes before the launch, most of the aircraft had been armed with air-to-ground rockets, heavy iron bombs, and other ordnance. Most of the aircraft were still located on the aft part of the flight deck. Suddenly, a Zuni high-velocity aircraft rocket (HVAR) located in a four-rocket pod on an F-4 Phantom ignited. Incredibly, it was a repeat of the disaster that occurred aboard the carrier U.S.S. *Forrestal* just 18 months earlier. The Zuni was a proven tactical weapon against ground targets, but had earned a reputation for being unstable and unsafe during intense flight deck operations.

At 8:19 A.M. the Phantom was parked on the port side aft awaiting its turn in the launch sequence when its Zuni blew up and, in a rapidly evolving chain reaction, other aircraft and their weapons began to burn and explode savagely. Pilots in their cockpits ejected and others jumped into the sea to avoid the rivers of burn-

An aerial photograph of the aft flight deck of the *Enterprise* after the fire was out. At least four huge craters in the deck—the result of bomb explosions—are visible. *USNI*

ing jet fuel and explosions. Several men were blown overboard, and within 20 minutes the aft one-third of the flight deck was a blazing inferno punctuated by major-caliber bomb detonations and aircraft exploding. The ship's commanding officer, Captain Kent L. Lee, turned the burning carrier into the wind to keep the billowing smoke off the deck thus providing firefighters and would-be rescuers the best possible chance for beating down the inferno.

Escorting destroyers U.S.S. *Bainbridge* DLGN-25, U.S.S. *Stoddard* DD-566, and U.S.S. *Rogers* DD-876 were assigned roles of search and rescue or fire fighting. The *Rogers* approached the port side aft of the burning ship and plied half a dozen fire hoses on the blaze. This was not a safe location for an escort. Explosions often damaged ships that attempted to fight fires aboard carriers, yet the *Rogers* remained on station despite the risk.

By 9 A.M., most of the aircraft and muni-

tions had either burned or detonated, and the fire-fighting crews began to gain the upper hand in the fight to save the ship. Foam foggers and water smothered the fires on deck. From below, word was passed that fires in the crew's livings quarters just under the flight deck were under control.

By 11:40 A.M., all fires were out and crews were shoving the smoldering wreckage on the flight deck over the side. The damage was horrific and reminiscent of the previous flight deck fires aboard the U.S.S. *Forrestal* and World War II aircraft carriers U.S.S. *Franklin* CV-13 and U.S.S. *Bunker Hill* CV-17. A number of large jagged cavities created by bomb explosions punctured the armored flight deck; the largest one was 15 feet by 20 feet. There were various splits in the deck, all caused by nine major-caliber bomb detonations. Further damage was prevented when exposed bombs were either hosed down or

The huge carrier steams at full speed to Pearl Harbor to allow the injured to be taken to Tripler General Army Hospital. *Navy League*

One of the bomb craters on the deck of the *Enterprise*. Her armored deck prevented the ship from being destroyed. *Author's Collection*

thrown overboard. The crew behaved with discipline and bravery despite massive amounts of flying shrapnel. Some of the injured were hit by white-hot bomb fragments that entered the body and actually cauterized the wounds. Most were badly burned, and those who were not completely immobilized did everything possible to save their ship and fellow shipmates. Interestingly, several of the crew said that they felt no pain until it was over.

Before noon on January 14, 1969, the great ship changed course for Pearl Harbor. Tripler General Army Hospital had been alerted and the staff took action to receive and treat the injured, primarily those with burns.

Two of the escorting destroyers remained in the area looking for swimmers, and the other accompanied the ship back to Oahu.

In midafternoon, the big ship docked in Pearl Harbor and waiting ambulances took the injured to the 1,000-bed Tripler General Hospital. Twenty-eight men did not make it back. Most of the dead were those who were near the first explosion under the F-4 Phantom and others caught in the ensuing maelstrom.

The ship experienced $150 million in damage and lost 15 aircraft. Her nuclear reactors were unaffected and with some jury-rigged deck plating, it was possible that the *Enterprise* could have continued air operations within hours. The Newport News Shipbuilding and Drydock Company had done excellent work, and the armored flight deck had again proven its worth.

Epilogue

The fire and massive explosions aboard the U.S.S. *Enterprise* in 1969 were the last suffered aboard a supercarrier to date. Improved training, detailed safety techniques, and better fire-fighting equipment have reduced the overall risk of another catastrophe. However, an aircraft carrier during flight operations is still the most dangerous acreage in the world.

The U.S.S. *Enterprise* was given the most comprehensive overhaul in naval history (1991–1994) and refueled in late 1994. She is currently home-ported in Norfolk, Virginia, and is expected to serve well into the early twenty-first century.

The U.S.S. *Stoddard* DD-566, one of the ships escorting the *Enterprise* during the fire. The *Stoddard* searched for swimmers with the *Bainbridge*. TIM

A bow view of the old but state-of-the-art U.S.S. *Enterprise* at the Norfolk Navy Yard in the summer of 1997. There are five portholes up forward and three others in the captain's cabin taken from the U.S.S. *Enterprise* of World War II fame. *Author's Collection*

U.S.S. *Constellation* CVA-64
Major Fire During Construction

On December 19, 1960, a fire started on the hangar deck of the unfinished *Kitty Hawk*-class attack carrier U.S.S. *Constellation* CVA-64 while it was being fitted out at the New York Naval Shipyard. Generally, 4,000 personnel were assigned to the *Constellation*; however, only 2,500 civilian workers were aboard the carrier when the fire began. Sadly, in the day-long blaze, 50 workers were killed and scores injured, as well as $75 million in damages.

U.S.S. Constellation:
A Kitty Hawk-Class Attack Carrier

The U.S. Navy was extremely pleased with the supercarrier that originated with the U.S.S. *Forrestal* CVA-59. The 27,000-ton, war-built *Essex*-class carriers were not capable of handling the increasingly heavier and sophisticated aircraft being designed. The supercarrier could launch up to four aircraft at a time versus two for the *Essex* class. Just as important were the fuel bunkerage and supply capacity of the new carriers. The *Constellation* carried 5,624 tons of JP-5 jet fuel and 7,828

The *Constellation* burns dockside at the New York Navy Yard on December 19, 1960. Smoke pours from hundreds of main deck openings; small boats gather around the stricken ship to rescue swimmers and those who jumped to their decks. *TIM - SFCB*

tons of ship fuel. This amounted to three times the aviation fuel; 70 percent more fuel oil as well as 150 percent of ordnance over the *Essex* class.

The *Kitty Hawk* class displaced 80,800 tons full load and was 1,046 feet in length with a 252 maximum flight deck width. They were fossil-fuel-driven ships that employed steam boilers and four geared turbines, which generated 280,000 shaft horsepower. The top speed was 30 plus knots. The U.S. Congress balked at the additional $100 million needed for a nuclear power plant (U.S.S. *Enterprise* CVAN-65), and the Navy ultimately had to settle for eight less-expensive variations of the *Forrestal* class. The *Constellation* was the fifth of these conventionally powered carriers.

The *Constellation* carried an air wing of 70 aircraft of all kinds, and for close-in defense was armed with Sea Sparrow missiles and later the Vulcan Phalanx 20-millimeter CIWS. As with all supercarriers, her deck was armored, and the latest in fire-fighting and damage-control systems were built in.

Utilizing experience gained in World War II, the Navy used fire-resistant paint, fireproof mattresses, and nonflammable lifejackets. Even

An overhead photo of the *Constellation* as she burns. By now a ten-alarm fire response is in action and many of the civilian workers have abandoned the ship. A light snow has just fallen. *TIM - SFCB*

The *Constellation* is ready to be commissioned into the U.S. Navy on October 27, 1961. After joining the fleet, her air wing exercised and become carrier qualified for combat. *TIM - SFCB*

the 300 miles of electric wire insulation aboard the ship was rendered almost fireproof. This class was fitted with overlapping and redundant fire-fighting systems that could literally flood the flight and hangar decks with foam fog and dense water spray. The fire-fighting system could be triggered and controlled from remote locations, yet unfortunately, the *Constellation* had not reached the point in her construction where these systems worked. It was planned that these systems would be activated and tested after she was in the fitting-out basin.

The keel for the *Constellation* was laid down at the New York Navy Yard on September 14, 1957, and three years later she was launched and christened on October 8, 1960. The following day she was towed to another berth for final work. At 10:30 A.M. on December 19, 1960, a fire began on the hangar deck and as the sophisticated fire fighting system was not yet operational, only hand fire extinguishers were available. It quickly spread before outside help could arrive. Interestingly, it was the forty-third fire aboard the carrier since construction had begun.

The combination of flammable material, welders, and careless workers often causes fires during the construction of large vessels. The previous 42 fires were minor, extinguished without outside help, and did not signify serious potential problems.

Fire on the Hangar Deck

The *Constellation* was crowded with civilian workers and Navy staff on the morning of December 19, 1960, the day the fire occurred. The Navy was anxious to get the new carrier to sea and on station. There was a commitment to maintain a minimum of three attack carriers each in the Mediterranean and the western Pacific. To date, local commanders were able to rotate supercarriers from one fleet to another to provide at least one ship able to launch nuclear-weapon-capable bombers. Having the *Constellation* available would improve the situation, so the Navy was exhorting the shipyard to a maximum effort.

The shipyard was doing everything possible to maintain pace and promised that the ship would be commissioned by early March 1961. In the last stages of construction, the flight and hangar decks were literally covered with excess debris, including much wooden scaffolding and pallets. Workers simply used

them as necessary and left them for cleanup crews later.

At 10:30 A.M., a civilian forklift driver, attempting to shove the steel forks under a pallet holding a trash dumpster, pushed against a piece of steel plating located on a pallet behind the dumpster. The pallet was out of sight of the workman, and by continuing to push the dumpster, the steel plate in turn progressively moved toward the bottom of a nearby 500-gallon fuel tank. The fuel tank contained diesel fuel oil used to test generators and other diesel engines utilized on the hangar deck. Finally, the steel plate was shoved too far. It came in contact with the brass drain valve under the tank. This valve was not properly screwed in and when investigated later looked as if it had been hammered as a last resort to seal it. The drain valve was sheared off, and fuel oil began to flow out on deck. A frightened worker ran to the flight deck and found a naval officer, Lt. Vito Milano, who was in charge of hull construction. Milano followed the worker down to the tank and saw that much of the fuel had drained onto the second deck through a bomb elevator and a series of holes cut for pipes and wiring in the deck. Milano attempted to plug the drain hole, but flames suddenly leaped up from below. A welder was working in a compartment under the hangar deck, and the river of diesel oil flowing by him ignited. Flames spread everywhere and began to feed on wooden scaffolding, plywood, and pallets that seemed to be everywhere.

The fire quickly spread throughout a number of lower deck compartments, temporarily trapping men by the hundreds. Wooden shacks and other debris on the hangar deck caught fire as well, and noxious fumes spread throughout the ship. Many of the compartments became ovens as the fires burned around them, yet wisely some of the men trapped in these compartments sealed watertight doors and waited for the fires to consume all nearby flammable materials before they moved on. Several men survived by just waiting and avoiding poisonous gasses and fumes. Others clamored to get off the burning carrier any way possible. Several jumped into the icy waters of the East River, while others boarded a barge alongside the ship and awaited a tug to pull it away to safety. In one way or another, about 2,500 workers attempted to leave the ship, fight fires, and remain out of harm's way. Not all would succeed.

By 10:40 A.M., the Brooklyn Navy Yard Fire Department was en route to the ship and a general alarm had sounded aboard the *Constellation*. Navy yard firemen attempted to board the ship but an onrush of escaping workers clogged the two main access gangways. Finally, fire and rescue workers boarded and assessed the severity of the fire. It had spread to many lower decks and compartments and was sweeping the hangar. The firefighters requested assistance from the New York Fire Department that ultimately initiated a ten-alarm fire response with 350 men and 120 pieces of heavy equipment.

Dockside fires were nothing new to local fire authorities. In a similar incident on February 9, 1942, the 83,423-ton French superliner S.S. *Normandie* caught fire very much like the *Constellation* and eventually turned over at her berth.

The local fire departments were determined that this was not going to happen with the nation's newest supercarrier. By noon, firefighters advanced on the inferno below decks and slowly brought the blaze under control. Shipyard workers were still exiting the ship and as the firefighters moved among the decks, they occasionally heard tapping on the walls. After opening the watertight doors, the firefighters freed more workers, but unfortunately in others, the men discovered bodies. Thick smoke and fumes shrouded the deck and made rescue efforts difficult and at times impossible. In fact, the fires did not hamper the firefighters—the smoke and overall lack of familiarity with the ship did.

By 2 P.M., cranes had lifted the dead and seriously injured off the ship and firefighters kept moving below decks spraying hot areas. By this time, the ship began to list due to the huge amounts of water pumped aboard, and when she reached 2 degrees to starboard, the Navy ordered the sea cocks on the port side opened to counter-flood the list.

Firefighters maintained their advance on the blaze below decks and by 10:46 P.M., the fire was declared under control. Over 12 hours had elapsed since the diesel tank leaked and a welder's torch ignited the fire. Workers went back aboard the following day to clean up and repair, but it was not for a few more days that all the smoldering remnants of the fire were finally out.

Epilogue and Aftermath

Fifty men lost their lives in the December 1960 fire. The ship, scheduled for delivery to the Navy three months later, did not reach the fleet until October 27, 1961—seven months beyond the anticipated date. Damage to the hangar and below-deck areas was extensive and the fire damaged a considerable amount of electric wiring. The intense heat warped much shell plating and interior bulkheads.

The cause of the fire was deemed accidental, but the fact that the ship was so extensively burned was laid at the feet of poor housekeeping and too much wood and other flammable material lying about. Better disposal of excess materials was called for as well as metal construction scaffolding. Safety procedures were reviewed, and improved onboard fire-fighting capability was initiated.

The *Constellation* went to sea in late 1961 and participated in operations all over the world including Vietnam. Currently, she is based out of San Diego, California, and as she is one of a dying breed of fossil fuel carriers, her retirement is imminent. Like those carriers that awaited her deployment in 1961, she awaits the construction of another nuclear-powered *Nimitz*-class carrier. Her next home port will be the carrier graveyard as part of the Pacific Reserve Fleet in Bremerton, Washington.

U.S.S. *Oriskany* CVA- 34
Forward Hangar Deck Fire

On October 26, 1966, a fire began in the flare locker aboard the *Essex*-class carrier U.S.S. *Oriskany* CVA-34. Forty-four men were killed including 24 veteran pilots who had survived countless missions over Vietnam only to die in their staterooms.

U.S.S. Oriskany: *An Essex-Class Carrier*

The U.S.S. *Oriskany* was laid down at the New York Navy Yard on May 1, 1944, and launched on October 13, 1945, just weeks after the conclusion of World War II. There was a huge surplus of fleet aircraft carriers, thus the unfinished *Oriskany* was laid up and all work suspended until October 1, 1947.

At war's end, it was obvious that jet aircraft would supplant propeller-driven naval fighters and bombers. This meant that existing carriers would have to be modernized to carry the new aircraft, and the first was the *Oriskany*. On September 25, 1950, she was commissioned and was the sole *Essex* attack carrier to be completed under the SCB-27A guidelines.

The *Oriskany* displaced 39,800 tons full load and was 888.5 feet in length with a flight deck width of 147.8 feet. She mounted eight 5-inch/38-caliber guns and numerous 3-inch/50-caliber guns for antiaircraft defense. She was powered by eight steam boilers and turbines that generated 150,000 shaft horsepower. At maximum speed, her four screws could drive the carrier at 33 knots. She had a crew totaling 1,531 with an air group of 831 officers and men. The *Oriskany* carried the full range of available jet-powered naval aircraft (like the F-9F Panther) and the more advanced piston-engine aircraft such as the AD-6 Skyraider.

After commissioning, the new carrier carried out a number of deployments, including Korea during 1952 and 1953. By the mid-1950s many of her sisters had an angled flight

An aircraft has just been launched from the *Oriskany* in this photo taken on July 12, 1960. A rescue helicopter stands by off her starboard side. *TIM*

On September 28, 1959, the *Essex*-class carrier U.S.S. *Oriskany* CVA-34 steams at high speed off the Pacific coast of California with a *Fletcher*-class destroyer in her wake. The *Oriskany* has now been rebuilt with an angled deck, steam catapults, and hurricane bow. *TIM - SFCB*

deck and an enclosed "hurricane" bow. It was time for the *Oriskany* to have a facelift, and in September 1957 she entered the San Francisco Naval Shipyard for a major overhaul. On March 7, 1959, the *Oriskany* was again commissioned and rejoined the fleet. For the next half decade she operated as part of the Pacific Fleet, spending more and more time off the Southeast Asian coastline. As the Vietnam War escalated, so did the contribution of the *Oriskany*. By October 1966, her air groups mounted over 20,000 successful sorties against the enemy and in one period, for which she

received the Navy Unit Commendation, her aircraft dropped nearly 10,000 tons of ordnance on enemy positions.

In mid-1966, the carrier steamed for Dixie Station, a featureless ocean grid square off Vietnam. From this area, strikes were launched on a 24-hour basis. In early July, she moved to the Tonkin Gulf and another ocean zone aptly named Yankee Station. This was another popular departure area for Task Force 77 aircraft heading for combat over Vietnam. Yankee Station was 18 degrees above the equator, thus the weather was hot and humid with intermittent rainstorms, especially during the monsoon season. So it was on October 26, 1966, when just after midnight six Skyraiders and seven Skyhawks were preparing for a strike.

Fire in the Forward Hangar: October 26, 1966

Air Wing 16 aviators had been scheduled to launch just after midnight on October 26, 1966, yet inclement weather made flight operations impossible. Thirteen aircraft had been prepared and spotted for launch, but it was decided that a launch would take place in daylight seven hours later. The time for the next launch was set at 7:30 A.M. To weary flight deck crews this meant that planned ordnance had to be removed and stowed. This included many Mark-24 Model 3 flares that had to be detached and stowed on waiting skids. Later the skids would be struck below in preparation for the morning launch.

The Mk-24 flare was a parachute flare that could provide up to 2 million candlepower for three minutes. Its chemical composition was magnesium and sodium nitrate and when ignited burned furiously at a tem-

The U.S.S. *Hamner* DD-718, which stood by to aid the stricken carrier. *Author's Collection*

perature of 4,500 degrees Fahrenheit. This temperature level was far greater than anything else aboard ship and would exceed even the most sophisticated fire-fighting tools and efforts. The residue from a burning flare was

Firefighters help with a hose that is being used on the hangar deck and below to contain the quickly spreading fire. *USNI*

Crews carry or trundle bombs and other flammable objects to the aft part of the flight deck or simply throw them over the side during the fire. *Author's Collection*

A crew throws a heavy-caliber bomb over the side from the sponson just aft from where the fire is raging. *USNI*

toxic and a deadly killer. The ship's designers had not anticipated storing and handling large numbers of this type of flare, thus there were no previously designated storage compartments. As a matter of practicality, a location five decks below the hangar bay, compartment A-606-A, was reserved for storage of these pyrotechnics. Another compartment, A-107-M, was unofficially selected due to its closer proximity to the flight deck. This second location was in the forward hangar bay and easily accessible to the flight deck. It was here that crews stored the flares removed from the 13-plane strike until needed a few hours later. Unfortunately, A-107-M was also above a number of officer staterooms where several veteran pilots lived.

Seaman Apprentice John Gervais was responsible for removing the flares and striking them below in compartment A-107-M, the unofficial flare locker. He worked until 6 A.M., muscling skids loaded with flares down to the locker's entrance. As the night watch ended, he looked forward to being relieved and going to morning chow. He closed and locked the door to the flare locker and headed for the mess.

Apprentice Airman James Sider was in charge of the flare locker on the day shift, a dubious responsibility. When he came on duty at 7 A.M. he saw 70 flares still on skids and realized that the watch was to begin with backbreaking labor. To make matters worse, the carrier was going to receive additional ordnance from a supply ship (an operation known as an "unrep," for underway replenishment), which would include even more flares for inventory and storage. He voiced his complaint to the leading petty officer who was less than sympathetic. Finally, Sider was able to convince a fellow sailor, George James, to assist in stowing the flares. The skids were moved to the doorway of A-107-M and in relays, James passed flares to Sider who placed them in the locker. Initially this worked fine, yet as James moved farther from the doorway to other skids, it became necessary to toss the flares rather than hand-deliver them. This shortcut proved fatal.

At about 7:15 A.M., one of the flares James threw to Sider caught its lanyard on a protrusion of sorts. James naturally tugged on the flare and the ignition sequence began with a "pop" that both James and Sider heard. The flare ignited as it fell to the steel deck outside the locker. James immediately panicked and fled. Sider, knowing that a serious problem had developed, picked up the burning flare and he too became consumed with fear, so much so that logic and safety concerns deserted him. Rather than allowing the flare to burn its three minutes or throw it over the side of the ship, he did the worst possible thing—he threw it into the flare

The carriers *Franklin D. Roosevelt* and *Constellation* maneuver to assist the burning *Oriskany*, seen in the distance. *Author's Collection*

locker that contained 650 stored flares. He secured the door with its dog handles and ran into the open hangar bay, shouting a warning, "Fire!" By 7:18 A.M., the fate of the ship had been sealed. The blazing flare ignited others in A-107-M that in turn caused a conflagration, which generated massive amounts of toxic fumes. The fumes entered the ship's forward ventilation system. Fire and toxic fumes engulfed the ship forward.

An escorting destroyer stops to inspect a life raft thrown from the *Oriskany*. *Author's Collection*

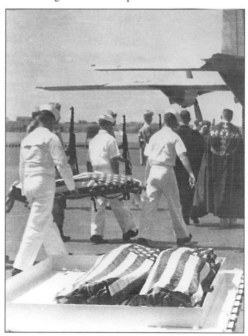

Some of the 44 dead are taken aboard aircraft and flown back to the United States. *Author's Collection*

The *Oriskany* as she sits at the now decommissioned Mare Island Naval Shipyard in Vallejo, California, in late 1997. As of early 1998, her future was still uncertain. *Author's Collection*

On December 11, 1954, Mrs. James V. Forrestal, widow of the first secretary of defense, christens the carrier named for her husband. This was the U.S. Navy's first supercarrier and revolutionized naval aviation. *Author's Collection*

The fire and fumes immediately affected 18 spaces below deck, including 11 officer staterooms. Events quickly took over and went beyond the efforts of men on the scene. Henry Brooks, hangar safety petty officer, rushed to the forward hangar bay and instructed others to throw a skid load of flares over the side at once. He then notified the bridge.

The quartermaster receiving the call at first thought it was a drill and so announced it over the loudspeaker. He quickly corrected himself and advised the ship's personnel that there was a fire and it was no drill. Captain John Iarrobino, the *Oriskany's* commanding officer, arrived on the bridge and quickly gave instructions to turn the ship to starboard to improve visibility through the heavy smoke. Five minutes had now gone by since the first warning, and officers in their staterooms below the flare locker were already dying in their sleep.

Moments later, "general quarters" was sounded to put all the crew at their stations. Explosions began to shake the ship forward as firefighters attempted to bring the fire under control or at least determine its extent. By 8 A.M., the fire forward had reached a critical stage and was literally sweeping through one compartment after another, either burning everything flammable or consuming all of the oxygen. In the next minutes, the ship was turned to port and then back to starboard to assist the fire-fighting operation. The fire had spread far beyond the confines of the flare locker and was causing subsidiary fires in overhead wiring and finally, at 8:42 A.M., it appeared that the firefighters had the upper hand. They were beginning to bring the fire under control. As a further precaution, ammunition magazines down several decks were flooded before they reached an unsafe temperature. In the hour that ensued, the fire-fighting teams gained control and just as they were about to declare victory, several 55-gallon paint drums located in the number one elevator pit burst into flame. A maximum effort was required to bring this new inferno under control as fire and more fumes found their way into crew spaces. Twenty minutes later, the fire was again under control.

For the next two hours, until 11:58 A.M., various small fires flashed up, but by noon, the fire was out. Now it was time to assess the damage and more important, the loss of life. Carriers U.S.S. *Franklin D Roosevelt* CVA-42 and U.S.S. *Constellation* CVA-64 provided medical assistance as destroyers including the U.S.S. *Hamner* DD-718 stood by.

Aftermath of an Inferno: Why, How, and Who?

The tragedy killed 8 enlisted men and 36 officers; 3 enlisted men died at their general quarters station. The remaining 5 enlisted men died in the public affairs office under the elevator pit. They were trapped and could not escape. Of the 36 officers, 24 were veteran pilots who faced death daily over Vietnam but died in their staterooms due to lack of oxygen, smoke poisoning, and burns. There were men who survived, but these incidences were rare.

The fault was placed partially on the unsanctioned use of a compartment for the storage of highly flammable pyrotechnics. Had the flight deck crew stored the flares in designated areas, the risk would have been reduced. Also, training or the lack of training was named as a cause as well as the improper handling of the flares by the two seamen. Leadership was also faulted as was the lack of adequate fog foam fire-fighting equipment.

Studies were initiated and changes made throughout the carrier fleet as a result of this tragedy. As to the *Oriskany*, she was refitted and rejoined the fleet on July 16, 1967. Her aircraft flew thousands of additional strikes over Vietnam, and nine years later she was mothballed. In 1998 she sat partially scrapped alongside a wharf in the decommissioned Mare Island Shipyard in Vallejo, California. The shipbreakers that purchased her went bankrupt, and her hulk awaited a new scrap dealer.

U.S.S. *Forrestal* CVA-59
Flight Deck Inferno

U.S.S. Forrestal:
First of the Supercarriers

The U.S.S. *Forrestal* had its origins in the post–World War II need for nuclear-bomb-capable aircraft that could strike anywhere in the world. The newly formed Air Force immediately laid claim to this task, yet the Navy had already initiated planning for a new type of aircraft carrier capable of fulfilling this role.

In the mid-1940s, atomic bombs were large clumsy objects that required a substantial aircraft for delivery. The Navy's AJ-1 Savage was the aircraft of choice, but an extensive reinforced flight deck was also necessary for an intended takeoff area of over 600 feet. The *Essex*-class attack carriers and the new *Midway* class were unsuitable, so a new carrier type was required.

Most national defense strategists theorized that World War III would probably be fought in the stratosphere and nuclear weapons would be as common as the iron bomb or artillery shells. Which service would be selected to deliver these weapons became a bitter contest between the Navy and the Air Force. The Navy appeared to have prevailed by 1948 when it received funding and authority to build the first supercarrier—the U.S.S. *United States* CVB-58. Unfortunately, the funding was revoked five days into construction and transferred to the Air Force for the development of the B-36 strategic bomber. The U.S.S. *United States* was sunk before it was launched. However, the Navy did not give up on the idea of the supercarrier. It would take a small, conventional war to pry funding from the U.S. Congress for the new carrier.

In 1950, North Korea invaded its neighbor, South Korea. The United States was committed to the United Nations' defense of South Korea, and the president asked, "Where is the nearest carrier?" Thus the advent of the supercarrier was assured.

Higher takeoff and landing speeds with aircraft that would ultimately be nine times heavier (1941 F-4F Wildcat—8,100 pounds—versus 1972 F-14 Tomcat—73,250

The U.S.S. *Forrestal* CVA-59 at sea shortly after being commissioned. Chiefly designed to carry the nuclear-bomb-capable A-3D Skywarrior, her deck also sports a number of aircraft types including the rugged propeller-driven AD Skyraider. *Author's Collection*

Flight deck damage-control personnel attempt to quench flames on the aft port side of the *Forrestal* on the morning of July 29, 1967. The fire has already burned several aircraft beyond recognition. *USNI*

pounds) necessitated a whole new concept. The supercarrier was born and exceeded the relatively modern *Midway* class by 15,000 tons, which alone was the displacement of an early World War II attack carrier. The U.S.S. *Forrestal*, whose motto is *Fidelity, Integrity, and Dignity*, was laid down at the Newport News Shipbuilding and Drydock Company on July 14, 1952; launched on December 11, 1954; and commissioned on October 1, 1955. She was designed from the keel up with an angled (canted) deck, hurricane bow, armored deck, and steam catapults. Her mast could be lowered to allow her to pass under bridges, and her cost was $189.9 million. She was 1,036 feet in length and her flight deck was 252 feet in width. She was the first carrier built without internal elevators—there were four deck-edge lifts. Her steam turbines provided 260,000 shaft horsepower, and the new carrier was honeycombed with 1,240 watertight compartments for passive defense. By comparison, the *Essex* class had 750 watertight compartments.

Her designed purpose was to carry nuclear-armed aircraft and the 83,500-pound A-3D Skywarrior was selected for this role. This role was never fulfilled as the Navy has not used any nuclear weapons to date, and the Skywarrior is now a museum piece. The *Forrestal* was armed with eight rapid-fire 5-inch/54-caliber guns located in galleries alongside her flight deck. These were later replaced by missiles and the Vulcan Phalanx 20-millimeter CIWS for antiair defense. The *Forrestal* was a formidable addition to U.S. sea power. She represented a quantum leap into the future of naval aviation and formed the design foundation for the carriers of today. The *Nimitz*-class (CVAN) nuclear supercarriers can trace their heritage to the *Forrestal*.

The Forrestal *at Sea with the Fleet*

The new carrier was in a class of its own, and aviators had to be trained to land and take off from such a ship. After her initial shakedown cruise and after minor repairs and improvements were made, her first major task

Fires that started when a Zuni rocket misfired and struck another plane's external fuel tank are nearly out. To the far right, the foremast of the destroyer U.S.S. *Rupertus* DD-851 can be seen as she maintains station alongside the stricken carrier. *USNI*

was to orient pilots to her huge flight deck. A number of training exercises were conducted off the eastern seaboard before she was forward-deployed into the eastern Atlantic and Mediterranean. The *Forrestal* was called upon to provide support in the Suez Crisis in November 1956 and again in the Lebanon Crisis in July 1958.

During the intervening years and until the Vietnam War began in earnest, the primary role of this carrier was to visit the major ports of the Old World. Each visit fully demonstrated the increased power of the United States and its Navy. No nation had ever built such a large combat vessel, and with her 79,000-ton full load displacement and 80 or more aircraft, this carrier was the most powerful warship in the world. The significance of this was not lost on our allies nor our potential enemies, the Soviet Union and related bloc countries.

During 1965 and into 1966, the *Forrestal* was given a major overhaul that included the installation of the NTDS (Naval Tactical Data System). NTDS was the first successful attempt to control air defense and friendly aircraft on strike missions in one integrated electronic system. First used on the U.S.S. *Oriskany* CVA-34, the NTDS proved to be highly satisfactory. Aside from providing the fleet with an electronic control umbrella, it also served as one of the major precursors to the AEGIS system currently in use. Rather than rejoining the Atlantic fleet after her overhaul, the *Forrestal* was transferred to the western Pacific (WestPac) for combat operations off the Vietnamese coast. The Vietnam War was escalating and the need for attack carriers was critical. The *Forrestal* was just one of many Atlantic Fleet carriers routinely conscripted for duty on Yankee Station. She arrived on July 25, 1967, and began sending her aircraft on combat missions over Vietnam.

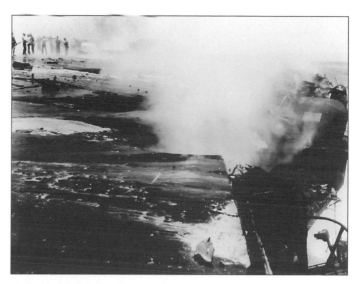

Still-smoldering bomb craters can be seen on the burned-out aft port side. The 5-inch gun mounts on the port side were destroyed and permanently removed during her subsequent refit. *USNI*

July 29, 1967: Fire on the Flight Deck

Having been on station for four days, the *Forrestal* successfully launched 150 missions without loss or mishap. Steaming 150 miles off the Vietnamese coastline, an early-morning mission was launched, and at 11 A.M. a second launch was scheduled. Lt. Commander John S. McCain III (a U.S. senator from Arizona) prepared to be launched in an A-4 Skyhawk for this second mission, when at 10:53 A.M. another A-4 exploded in front of his aircraft. Ironically he had also been aboard the U.S.S. *Oriskany* during the tragic fire just 10 months earlier and had transferred to the *Forrestal* to continue his duty at sea. The A-4 was now engulfed in flames and the pilot, Lt. (jg) David Dollarhide attempted to get out and away from the raging inferno. He broke his hip in the attempt but his plane captain rescued him.

An A-4 Skyhawk, loaded with 1,700 gallons of fuel (800 internal and 900 gallons external tank) accidentally had spewed some excess fuel in a "hot start," and the resulting flame in turn torched a nearby pod of Zuni rockets on a waiting F-4 Phantom strike fighter. The Zuni was a 110-inch-long, 5-inch-diameter high-velocity aircraft rocket capable of 1,400 knots. It could be used for air-to-ground or air-to-air combat. When its war-

Damage-controlmen roll and push heavy-caliber bombs over the side from the hangar deck below the blazing flight deck. This prevented a greater tragedy. *USNI*

head was set for point detonation, it was lethal. The F-4 Phantom mounted a pod of these missiles and when one was heated, it self-launched and streaked across the flight deck to hit the 900-gallon external fuel tank of Lt. Dollarhide's Skyhawk. The effect was devastating as flaming jet fuel spread over the deck. The growing fires set off other ordnance being prepared for the upcoming strike. Ultimately the entire aft part of the flight deck was a scene

Helicopters from all over the region take the severely injured and dead ashore to a hospital at the Da Nang Navy Base in South Vietnam. *Author's Collection*

The remains of a burned-out aircraft are examined after the fire was completely extinguished. *Author's Collection*

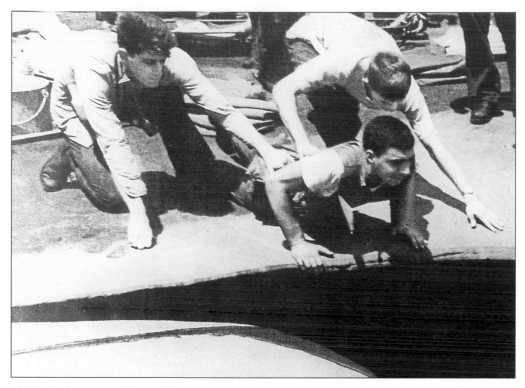

Flight deck personnel peer down into one of the bomb craters to inspect the damaged area. The armored deck is easily seen and as hoped it provided protection to the ship. *Author's Collection*

of flames, choking smoke, cooked-off ammunition, and exploding bombs. Men attempted to bring the fires under control and threw bombs and rockets over the side before they too exploded and further compounded the tragedy. Lt. Commander McCain; another pilot, Lt. Commander Herbert Hope; Lt. (jg) Robert Cates; and many others assisted the wounded and dying.

The 750-pound bombs detonated aft and blew holes through the thickly armored flight deck. Before this could be stopped, flaming fuel and additional bombs fell through the now-jagged holes in the deck and exploded below to a depth of six additional decks. Men were killed instantly on the aft flight deck; 50 men were killed below, and others were blown over the side of the smoking ship. Some of the bombs did not immediately explode and hours later men were lowered by rope to defuse them before a new round of destruction began.

On the flight deck, unimaginable feats of bravery became the norm. Men who were severely wounded begged to be allowed to continue helping others, and one 130-pound officer picked up a 250-pound bomb with

seeming ease and threw it over the side. Within minutes of the initial explosions, damage-control teams attacked the blaze and fellow carriers U.S.S. *Oriskany* CVA-34 and U.S.S. *Bon Homme Richard* CVA-34 rendered assistance by sending their helicopters to pick up injured men for treatment. Added to the rescue effort were helicopters from the Navy base at Da Nang, which flew out to evacuate the severely injured.

It was early evening before crews contained the fire on the flight deck, and several hours later before they controlled or extinguished the large number of subsidiary blazes down below. The gruesome task of locating and identifying the dead would take days.

The death toll was staggering. The explosions had killed 134 men and injured or badly burned hundreds of others. Twenty-one aircraft were completely destroyed and another 43 damaged beyond the repair facilities of the carrier. In essence, the *Forrestal's* air wing was gone, and the carrier had suffered major damages that would require an extensive and expensive ($72 million) repair. The carrier was finished as a viable combat platform and was detached from

An aerial view of the damage done to the aft flight deck of the *Forrestal*. *Author's Collection*

The flight deck shortly after the fire was out. This was one of the worst fires in naval aviation history. *Author's Collection*

Yankee Station. On her way back to the United States via the Subic Bay Naval Station in the Republic of the Philippines, the hospital ship U.S.S. *Repose* AH-16 met the burned-out carrier where a number of her wounded were transferred for treatment. The *Forrestal* put into Subic Bay for temporary repairs and then quietly left for the Norfolk Naval Shipyard for an extended refit. She arrived back home on September 14, 1967.

Epilogue

The damage to the *Forrestal* was studied as was that of the *Oriskany*, which had occurred less than a year earlier. In essence, heightened operations on Yankee Station and Dixie Station caused accidents, and the need for increased attention to safety was emphasized. Training was stressed in fire survival and ordnance handling. Bombs and rockets were made more stable. For future carrier designs and construction, all hangars are able to be divided into three separate compartments with fireproof doors. In addition, fireproof or

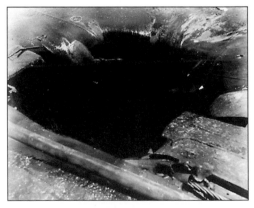

One of the craters caused by the explosions of seven heavy-caliber bombs. Some of the explosions penetrated three decks. *USNI*

fire-retardant materials are used wherever possible in construction. Fire is the greatest enemy of all combat vessels and in particular the aircraft carrier. Safety is now a primary concern and the modern carrier is constructed and operated with this as its foundation.

The destroyer U.S.S. *Rupertus* DD-851. This photo was taken before she was modernized. This ship stood by the burning *Forrestal* for three hours, maintaining station as close as 20 feet. The *Rupertus* fought fires, rescued jumpers, and cooled the magazines of the carrier's 5-inch guns. *TIM - SFCB*

CHAPTER FOUR

MYSTERIOUS AND CURIOUS

U.S.S. *Cyclops*, U.S. Navy Collier
Lost without a Trace

The U.S.S. *Cyclops*, a relatively modern collier and fleet service ship, failed to arrive in Baltimore, Maryland, as scheduled. The ship with her crew of 230 enlisted personnel, 20 officers, and 57 passengers left Bahia, Brazil, on February 21, 1918, in the late afternoon and arrived in Barbados on March 4, 1918. At 6 P.M. on the same day, she slowly steamed out of the island harbor for Baltimore where she was due on March 13. To this day, there has been no trace of the *Cyclops*.

The collier U.S.S. *Cyclops* shortly before her fateful trip to South America in February 1918. Her pilothouse is forward between two large masts. Captain Worley and Lt. Nervig spent evenings atop the box-like pilothouse chatting about the sea. *USNI*

The U.S.S. *Cyclops* rides at anchor in San Francisco Bay shortly after being commissioned as a U.S. Naval auxiliary. She was well equipped to coal warships; however, the increased use of the oil-fired boiler soon rendered this state-of-the-art collier obsolete. *Author's Collection*

The U.S.S. Cyclops: *A Neptune-Class Collier*

The U.S. Navy, like all pre-World War I navies, relied upon coal to power its ships. Without a dependable source of good, high-quality coal, a fleet became idle after a few days of operation. Recognizing this, the Navy sought to build ships designed exclusively for coaling, consequently the *Neptune* class was created, which included the *Cyclops*. These ships displaced a hefty 19,360 tons, were 542 feet in length with a 65-foot beam. On two screws, these colliers were capable of 15 knots.

William Cramp and Sons built the *Cyclops* in their Philadelphia yard and launched it on May 7, 1910. She began her career by supplying units of the Atlantic Fleet that were operating in the Baltic during the early summer of 1911. She returned to the east coast of the United States and, after a period in the eastern Caribbean, she was detached to provide coal to the fleet patrolling off Mexico.

Soon after the United States' entry into World War I, she was commissioned into the active naval service and on May 1, 1917, her civilian master, George W. Worley, became a Lt. Commander in the Reserve Force. After a trip to Europe, the ship returned from the war zone in July 1917, and for the next six months operated along the east coast of the United States. From here she was assigned to the Naval Overseas Transportation Service on January 9, 1918. Her first trip was to various ports in Brazil, and it would be her last trip.

The Last Days of the Cyclops *and Her Crew of 307 Men*

The *Cyclops* left Norfolk January 18, 1918, with a full load of coal, various stores, and mail for ships in the South American Patrol Fleet operating off Brazil. The trip, as told by Conrad A. Nervig, a temporary watch officer aboard the *Cyclops*, was uneventful but highly irregular. He was the only known survivor of the trip from Norfolk to South America aboard the *Cyclops*.

Captain Worley was considered the epitome of an uncultured, insecure, belligerent bully. His skill in navigation was rudimentary as was his ability as a ship handler. At least, this is how Nervig saw his commanding officer during the short voyage. Incident after incident seemed to

Launching day for the U.S.S. *Exploit* MSO-440 on April 10, 1951. Crews used this wooden-hulled minesweeper to locate what was suspected to be the wreck of the *Cyclops* on July 20, 1974. The wreck turned out to be that of another unidentified ship. *TIM - SFCB*

follow the ship south. There was a narrow escape with the U.S.S. *Survey* as the *Cyclops* was leaving Norfolk. Fortunately, a collision between the antisubmarine ship and the collier was avoided at the last minute. On January 13, 1918, Captain Worley placed his executive officer, Lt. Forbes, in hack (room arrest) over a minor argument on the ship's work assignments. Later that day the ship's doctor ordered Ensign Cain, a watch officer, to sick bay, an action taken to prevent the captain's wrath from being visited upon the young officer. Unfortunately, Ensign Cain had the midwatch, which then fell to Lt. Nervig. Nervig, understandably nervous, decided to make the best of it and at the appointed time, appeared on the bridge. Shortly thereafter, Captain Worley joined him, dressed in woolen underwear, derby hat, and carrying a cane. Nervig chalked this up to the fact that a captain at sea is regarded as "master after God," so his bizarre dress went unchallenged. For hours the Captain entertained Nervig with one sea story after another.

On January 22, 1918, the *Cyclops* arrived in Bahia Harbor, and was moored next to the U.S.S. *Raleigh*, a pre-war cruiser. Coal and stores were transferred, and the *Cyclops* exacted her toll by fouling the *Raleigh* twice while pulling away. The *Cyclops* then sailed for Rio de Janeiro where Nervig was to leave for the U.S.S. *Glacier*. Unfortunately, the trip from Bahia to Rio de Janeiro was slowed down by the starboard engine being disabled. Her high-pressure cylinder head blew off, and the port engine had to provide power for the trip.

The *Cyclops* discharged the balance of her cargo to hungry ships in the South American Patrol Squadron and for her return trip to the United States the collier was loaded with 10,000 tons of manganese ore.

The ship made a short stop in Barbados to fill her own coal bunkers for the journey to Baltimore. Promptly at 6 P.M. on March 4, 1918, the collier slowly moved away from the coal storage dock and out to sea. Strangely, the *Cyclops* sailed southward instead of north or at least northwest. The ship and the 307 souls aboard were never seen again. The collier simply disappeared.

Speculation on the Loss of the Cyclops

The ship had a 24-hour radio watch with adequate wireless telegraphy capability and was operating in well-defined coastal shipping lanes (or at least she was supposed to have been). The *Cyclops* was a well-found ship and capable of carrying high-density cargoes such as various types of ore. It is probable that her starboard engine was still disabled, and the collier was operating on one screw, thus her ability to maneuver was hampered.

The ship was loaded with manganese ore—a dense, heavy, and slightly magnetic material. If properly distributed in the holds, cargo of this nature would not present any problem to the ship's safety, but if not, disaster could result. The ship was fully laden to her plimsoll line, but due to the cargo weight, the lack of bulk in the hull was deceiving. As it is assumed that Lt. Forbes, the executive officer, was still in hack, it can be further assumed that an inexperienced cargomaster may have been assigned to load the ship. Following this line of reasoning, the ship could have been loaded in her fore and aft holds, the compactness of the manganese ore deceptively pulling the ship down to its fully laden status. Inexperience would account for this. Nervig felt this was the situation and theorized that the ship must have split in two halves, both of which immediately sank without a hint of flotsam or survivors. The ship's hull working amidships could have placed an unbearable strain that caused the ship to jackknife and sink. Plausible, but what caused the straw that broke the camel's back?

One explanation was that her cargo shifted, thus causing her to roll over and sink. This reasoning is not likely due to the nature of manganese and its stable nature—it settles to the bottom of the hold and does not normally shift.

Another speculation was that she encountered a freak storm and sank. This was virtually impossible as the hurricane season was several months distant and there was no report of any unfavorable weather in the region during the time period. There was no reported earthquake either under the sea or on land nor was any regional volcanic eruption noted that would have caused a "tsunami," or rogue tidal wave. The area in which she was to have sailed was not without shoals and small islands, but a grounding would have left some evidence, including survivors.

Two propositions are reasonably certain: the ship sank immediately (from whatever cause) and the sinking likely occurred in darkness, in the very early hours. The *Cyclops* probably disappeared under the sea so quickly that it prevented any lifeboat launching or distress signals. Her boats must have been unmanned and attached when she was lost. Except for the

bridge watch, posted lookouts (if any), and the engine room gang, the rest of the crew would have been in their hammocks or bunks asleep. No more than 25 to 40 men out of 307 would have been awake and on duty. The nature of a warship is one of having everything battened down and in its proper place, thus items that might have surfaced after the ship sank were at a very minimum and with prevailing currents would have swept far out to sea and eventual oblivion. The *Cyclops* was a warship and thus would have operated shrouded in darkness with most scuttles and portlights closed to prevent detection by German submarines or surface raiders. A rapid sinking would have prevented the vast majority of the crew from escaping and would have trapped items inside that might have otherwise escaped to the surface.

Having analyzed the various theories concerning the sinking of the *Cyclops*, it is quite conceivable that the ship broke in two halves and foundered within a few minutes in darkness. The sheer weight of a poorly distributed, highly dense cargo could drag a ship down quickly. The speed with which she sank tends to be supported by the lack of any evidence of her passing. Her crew was obviously down below; but in the tropics, it was the habit of many sailors to sleep on deck due to the humidity and heat below. The outside temperature in the Caribbean was an average of 80 degrees Fahrenheit even in March. This phenomenon may lend some support to the possibility that she was lost in more northerly waters closer to her destination.

As to whether she was torpedoed by a U-boat, German Naval authorities denied that any submarine or surface raider was operating in or near the *Cyclops*'s homeward track. Of course, as Captain Worley had become erratic, he could have taken them on any course and quite far from their intended cruising area. This scenario is highly unlikely, but it leads to another rather interesting theory.

Presuming a calm sea with no unusual wave action, something had to cause her hull to split in an area probably forward of the engine spaces. Torpedoes might have done this had they hit her amidships. By their very nature, a torpedo would have detonated upon hitting her side plating and not necessarily broken her back. The U.S.S. *Langley* CV-1, which was converted from a *Neptune*-class collier (U.S.S. *Jupiter*) was heavily bombed in February 1942 by the Japanese and had to be abandoned. To sink her, an escort-

The U.S.S. *Florikan* ARS-9, a sister ship to the U.S.S. *Kittiwake*, used as the dive ship for the suspected wreck of the *Cyclops* over the three-day period from July 30 to August 1, 1974. The wreck was not that of the old collier and an extended search also proved fruitless. *Author's Collection*

ing destroyer pumped nine 4-inch shells into her hull and then two 21-inch torpedoes. All of this failed to sink the hulk and she had to be left slowly sinking. The torpedo detonations were amidships and did not break her back. This leaves the theory of a drifting mine. If a mine exploded under her hull amidships, this could have broken her back and caused both halves of the ship to sink like stones.

Mine warfare was popular in the Allied navies, and minefields were sown around Rio de Janeiro and various ports along the American eastern seaboard. There is the possibility that a mine, especially one with a 500-plus-pound explosive could have broken loose and intercepted the *Cyclops*. Based on the presumption that the *Cyclops* sank immediately, an explosion of great force ruptured her hull, probably amidships, which in turn caused her to jackknife and sink. Captain Worley, with his unpredictable navigation skills, could very well have wandered into a mine field or in an area with ocean currents prone to collect mines that

had broken loose from their moorings. It was not unusual for ships to hit a mine and quickly sink. What was unusual was that there was no evidence left floating. Other less likely possibilities include a rogue wave or the ship bottoming on a shoal that caused her hull to rapidly snap. If the ship is ever discovered, it is likely that it will be found in two halves, the victim of an unbearable stress fracture in her hull.

To this day, the mystery of the lost collier haunts the U.S. Navy. As late as 1974, it was thought that the *Cyclops* had been discovered 70 miles off the Virginia coast in 180 feet of water. Accordingly, the U.S.S. *Exploit* MSO-440, a minesweeper with exceptionally sensitive navigational equipment, was able to locate the suspected wreck and mark it with a buoy. Not long thereafter, a dive team from the U.S.S. *Opportune* ARS-41, a submarine rescue unit, televised the wreck for analysis. It was firmly established that the wreck was not the *Cyclops*. A widened search produced no further evidence, and the mission was ended.

In reality, it is probable that no one will ever know the absolute truth, and the loss of the *Cyclops* will be one of the great unsolved mysteries of the sea. Perhaps underwater sensor technology will someday locate her remains and provide more answers or maybe more questions. She still remains the Navy's greatest mystery.

U.S.S. *Memphis* ACR-10
Unwitting Victim of a Tidal Wave

Birth of the Modern American Steel Cruiser

Cruisers dominated the sea campaigns of the Spanish-American War on both sides, and the influence of this ship type became a significant factor in future U.S. warship construction. The emergence of the U.S. Navy as the consummate victor in the Spanish-American War did not go unnoticed in the European naval community. However, Great Britain, the acknowledged naval leader, was more concerned with the efforts of potential adversaries on the continent. In response to new German, French, and Italian cruiser designs, Great Britain replied with the *Cressy* class of six ships built at the end of the nineteenth century. All were well-armed and armored ships capable of 21 knots, yet by the advent of World War I, were obsolete and pitifully defenseless against the submarine. H.M.S. *Cressy* and sisters *Aboukir* and *Hogue* all fell victim to torpedo attack from the U-9 on September 22, 1914, with the loss of 1,500 lives.

The *Cressy* class intrigued naval designers in the United States, and they built a series of large armored cruisers beginning with the *Pennsyl-vania* class in 1899 and culminating with the *Tennessee* (*Memphis*) class in 1902. In all, 10 ships were built that comprised the "big 10" cruisers in the U.S. Navy.

The last five of the *Tennessee* (renamed *Memphis*) class were the most modern and well equipped. This class included the U.S.S. *Washington* (*Seattle*) ACR-11, U.S.S. *North Carolina* (*Charlotte*) ACR-12, U.S.S. *Montana* (*Missoula*) ACR-13, and the U.S.S. *Tennessee* (*Memphis*) ACR-10. All were renamed when the Navy began building battleships that required the names of states; consequently, the armored cruisers were renamed for principal cities within the namesake states.

U.S.S. Tennessee *ACR-10*

The *Tennessee* class represented the best of the armored cruiser concept and coincidentally the last built by the U.S. Navy. They displaced 14,500 tons, had a length of 504.5 feet, and a beam of 72.8 feet. Their two vertical triple expansion engines generated a maximum of 26,963 shaft horsepower and drove the ship at 22.16 knots. They carried a mixed battery of 10-inch, 6-inch, 3-inch, and smaller weapons including four 21-inch hull mounted torpedo tubes. Typically the crew included 40 officers and 874 enlisted men.

The Navy awarded the Cramp Shipbuilding Company of Philadelphia, Pennsylvania, the contract to build the *Tennessee*. She was laid down on June 20, 1903; launched on December 3, 1904; and on July 17, 1906, the new armored cruiser was commissioned. After a period of sea trials and repairs to deficiencies identified by her new officers and crew, the ship entered active naval service.

Mid-1907 found the *Tennessee* in Europe for a short operation with the Special Service Squadron, and then back to the continental United States for assignment to the West Coast. Next she served off the east coast of the United States and the Caribbean until June 1911 when she was placed in reserve in the Portsmouth Naval Yard.

The impending war in Europe brought the *Tennessee* out of premature retirement again in May 1914, when she became a receiving ship at the New York Navy Yard. There she remained until called upon to escort the first American Relief Expedition to Europe in early 1915. In August of the same year, a crisis in a more familiar part of the world caused the cruiser to become reacquainted with the seemingly never-ending diplomatic and political problems of the Caribbean.

She acted as a troop ship carrying the 1st Regiment of the Marine Expeditionary to Haiti along with the Marine Artillery Battalion. The acting U.S. station ship in Haitian waters, the U.S.S. *Washington* (later U.S.S. *Seattle*) was in need of an overhaul, thus the *Tennessee* relieved her. Captain Edward Beach transferred from the *Washington* to assume command of the *Tenn-essee* due to his particular skill in regional diplomatic relations. A superb commander, he was to be the last active commanding officer of this fine vessel. The cruiser next returned to the United States for an overhaul, and on May 25, 1915, was renamed the U.S.S. *Memphis*. Problems in San Domingo, the Dominican

The U.S.S. *Tennessee* shortly after being launched. Her hull was white and her superstructure a buff color. She had a massive number of broadside guns, and as the great seismic-induced waves hit her, the shutters over the gun ports stove in or were simply torn loose. *TIM*

Republic, reached a boiling point in the summer of 1916. "Send in the Marines" was almost a commonplace sentiment in this region, and always accompanying the leathernecks was the U.S. Navy. In this new crisis, it was headed by the armored cruiser U.S.S. *Memphis*. On August 29, 1916, she was riding at anchor in Santo Domingo Harbor.

The Loss of the U.S.S. Memphis: *August 29, 1916—3 P.M. to 5 P.M.*

Captain Beach was not only a highly competent naval officer, but also a seaman. There is a difference, yet both qualities are absolutely essential for success in seaborne command. The Caribbean is known for its mercurial nature and ruthless treatment of ships and seafarers. One moment it is calm and peaceful and the next it is violent and unforgiving.

On the afternoon of August 29, 1916, the *Memphis* was riding at anchor in the open anchorage of Santo Domingo Harbor. The water was warm, the winds slight, and the only other warship in the roadstead was the U.S.S. *Castine*, a Spanish-American War relic. The depth of the water in which the ship was anchored was approximately 55 feet, and her anchor was strung out at 70 fathoms or 420 feet, which was an ideal length-to-depth ratio. The ship was several thousand yards from the shoreline of Santo Domingo. Only 2 of the 16 boilers were lit as instructed by standing policy from the force commander, Rear Admiral William Caperton.

A photo of a sister ship, the U.S.S. *Washington*, turned U.S.S. *Seattle*. The *Washington*, under the command of Captain Edward Beach, was replaced by the *Tennessee (Memphis)*, and Beach assumed command in order to provide needed diplomatic services in the region. *TIM*

The U.S.S. *California* (renamed U.S.S. *San Diego*) at anchor. Although slightly less in displacement, the *California* closely resembled the *Tennessee (Memphis)* in profile. Accordingly, this is probably what the *Memphis* looked like when the waves began to worsen. The rolling became so pronounced that her boat booms went under and then waves began to inundate her hull and superstructure. Later, bridge personnel took refuge within the forward cage mast, which is plainly visible on the *San Diego*. The *San Diego* was sunk by an underwater explosion in 1918. *TIM*

His theory was that two boilers would be sufficient to operate necessary machinery aboard ship while anchored, and other boilers could be lit off in time to deal with any emergency.

Many of the crew had gone ashore for recreation and the afternoon of Tuesday, August 29, was calm; at 79 degrees Fahrenheit the temperature was not as oppressive as was possible in the region.

Lt. Commander Yancey Williams, the *Memphis'* executive officer, was an excellent seaman, and as the afternoon watch began, he sensed a change in the sea state. Williams observed large swells outside the anchorage, something not overly unusual in an open roadstead. A quick check of the barometer showed

its reading at 30.09, which too was not unusual. However, Williams sensed impending danger from his continued observation of the sea and the growing size of the swells outside the harbor. He instructed the officer of the deck to have the launches recalled from the shore and then went below to advise the captain of his actions. It was now shortly after 1 P.M.

Mariners know that several hundred miles south of Santo Domingo there is a rather deep fault on the ocean floor and that any rock slippage can produce a disturbance of varying degree on the surface of the sea. At or about noon on August 29, 1916, it is generally known that a major shift on the sea bed occurred, initiating large swells on the surface.

107

A typical boiler room with open furnace doors aboard an early steel warship. Firemen and water tenders were tossed around in this area aboard the rolling *Memphis* and incredulously watched seawater roaring down the funnels to snuff out the fires. *Author's Collection*

They began moving toward Santo Domingo Harbor, which would receive their wrath five hours later. After being notified of his executive officer's suspicions, Captain Beach fully agreed upon coming up on deck and looking seaward. Something out of the ordinary was about to occur, and Beach immediately ordered that the ship be made ready for heavy weather. Into the late afternoon the officers and men of the *Memphis* labored to bring the ship to a state where she could sustain heavy seas, but nothing could be done to prevent the impending onslaught of mountains of water. Additional boilers were lit off by the engineers, but bringing the ship to a point where sufficient steam pressure was available was a matter

of time. By 3:50 P.M., the ship was rolling severely and the engineering staff was having great difficulty firing the boilers to bring up the needed steam.

The nearby gunboat *Castine* did have sufficient steam to move at a speed of 9 knots. Although slow, this speed was 9 knots faster than the *Memphis*, and adequate for an experienced seaman to weather most storms. Her commanding officer up anchored and began to maneuver in anticipation.

On the *Memphis,* the crew attempted to replace the shutters that protected the broadside mounted 6-inch guns. From 4 P.M. onward, Captain Beach first chided and then demanded steam so that the ship could slip her anchor and maneuver seaward. The engine room was having its own difficulties as water was beginning to flood downward through various air ducts and the severity of the ship's roll was not helping matters. At 4:15 P.M., the first major casualties occurred. The ship's launch, which was returning to the *Memphis*, foundered in the surf and dumped its occupants into the swirling sea. Tragically, 25 of the 31 occupants of this boat were lost in the surf. The *Castine* was also caught in the surf and it was doubted whether the old gunboat would survive the next series of waves.

Onboard the *Memphis*, the engineers toiled to bring up steam and by 4:35 P.M. the gauge stood at 90 psi. A frantic call from the bridge told the engine room that full power was needed as the ship was in imminent danger. The starboard engine room telegraph rang down full speed astern and the port telegraph rang down full astern. The engineers pleaded for five more minutes.

Captain Beach, who was fully versed in the habits of large swells, recognized that getting to sea and into deep water was the only salvation for his ship. For this, the engines had to respond. As this drama unfolded and the ship rolled with gunports under, the *Castine* chugged by afloat but a shambles. Her upper works were nonexistent, but she had survived the surf and was making her way to deep water.

The *Memphis* now began to strike the bottom of the anchorage with every major swell; throughout the ship the crew could feel a well-defined thud. The engine room still could not provide sufficient power for the ship to move and it was now 4:45 P.M. The ship had made one roll some 60 degrees and was now routinely striking bottom. This caused the hull to

A rare photo of the stranded cruiser within days after huge swells forced her ashore. Crews built a wooden plank bridge from the ship to the bluffs for access. *Author's Collection*

become distorted and moved the engines from their beds. Just as steam was coming up, the engine room filled with steam and water came down the funnels and put the fires out.

Just before 5 P.M., three successive waves struck the ship and literally cascaded down on her from above, filling the funnels, smashing the gunports, ripping out guard rails, and nearly drowning everyone aboard. Most of the men survived by being within the ship; those on the exposed deck had the worst experiences. By 5 P.M., the *Memphis* was alongside the beach and battered into a helpless wreck. There she would remain.

Epilogue

The *Memphis* had ceased to be a viable ship, and was being forcefully buffeted against the shore in 12 feet of water. However, she was still the haven for the majority of her 800-plus crew who were now just emerging from various precarious but relatively safe places all over the ship. It was time to abandon ship and get ashore as soon as possible. Two hundred—a quarter of the ship's company—were injured and had to be moved without delay. Crew members rigged a line ashore from a location on the cage mast forward several feet above the bridge. They soon rigged a number of hawsers and successfully moved the injured to dry land via canvas coal bags. After the wounded came the others and finally, after night had fallen, Captain Beach left his once beautiful command.

Forty-three of the *Memphis'* crew perished either aboard or in one of the launches. In all, 33 lost their lives in the boats that were smashed by the waves, 25 sailors alone in one boat that had just left the recreation dock on its journey back to the ship. The *Memphis* was no longer a ship as she now gently rocked back and forth less than 30 yards from the beach.

The fallout from this incident was as expected. Captain Beach was charged with negligence and inefficiency. He was found guilty and suffered the loss of five numbers on the promotion list. Yet the real punishment was being charged with an offense. It meant the end to a brilliant career. In June 1919, three years after the disaster, the secretary of the Navy cleansed his record in an act of true justice.

As for the *Memphis*, she was declared a total loss and the battleship U.S.S. *New Hampshire* was detailed to remove her guns and any useable equipment. On December 17, 1917, she was removed from the Navy's active list, and four years later on January 17, 1922, she was sold to A. H. Radetsky Iron and Metal Company of Denver, Colorado, for scrapping. For the next 15 years, the scrap company attempted to break up the hulk, but with little success. Finally, armed with modern ship-breaking machinery, the company broke up the *Memphis* and now little remains to mark the passing of the cruiser.

A photo of the *Memphis* in 1921 showing what the wave must have looked like as it struck the ship. The wave was so high that it poured down the funnels and doused the furnace fires. *TIM*

What was left of the ship after salvers from the older battleship U.S.S. *New Hampshire* stripped it of equipment. *Author's Collection*

U.S.S. *Pueblo* AGER-2
David versus Goliath

In the early 1960s, the U.S. military was obsessed with gathering intelligence on real and prospective enemies. One of these countries was and still is North Korea. The only difference between the present day and 1968, the year of the "Pueblo Incident," is that intelligence-gathering devices need not be within visual sight of the enemy.

In 1968, the U.S. Navy was capable of securing an amazing array of information. The problem was that it required loitering ships and aircraft passing close to international boundaries to get it. One such information-gathering ship was the U.S.S. *Pueblo* AGER-2. On January 23, 1968, her captain surrendered his ship to North Korean naval units operating off their coastline. The crew was freed a year later, yet the ship remains in Wonsan Harbor as a tourist attraction. What happened to this ship and its crew will forever occupy a prominent place among the U.S. Navy's more colorful and controversial historical events. It began in December 1966.

Commanding a Replica of the Ship Used in a World War II Comedy

Lt. Commander Lloyd "Pete" Bucher had been hoping for a submarine command or at least a medium-sized surface ship. Being ordered to assume command of an AKL, a 179-foot-long, 906-ton light coastal cargo ship, was not a choice career assignment. It was the same type of ship featured in the film *Mister Roberts*, and was described as an "old rust bucket." It was a command, however, and it was to be renovated into greater importance as an intelligence-gathering ship. She was powered by a 1,000-horsepower diesel engine turning two shafts at a maximum speed of 13 knots. These ships could venture into coves and inlets forbidden to larger draft cargo ships, making them ideal for localized Army

The U.S.S. *Pueblo* AGER-2 shortly after being commissioned at the Puget Sound Navy Yard. She was an ungainly ship that wallowed and rolled horribly even in a moderate sea. *USNI*

The *Pueblo* off San Diego conducts trials. The unusual ship passed all of her trials and was declared ready for sea. Her steering system was continually breaking down, however, with no technical assistance available for repairs. *TIM*

Soviet-built *P-4* fast torpedo boats of the North Korean Navy that came out of Wonsan Harbor to investigate the ship prowling off their coast. *TIM*

The *Pueblo* in Wonsan Harbor after being captured. This is a UP photo. The North Korean-run press used a photograph of the heavy cruiser *St. Paul* CA-73 as the *Pueblo*. *TIM*

operations. This class of ship normally carried a crew of 3 officers and 24 enlisted men. The U.S. Army had used the U.S.S. *Pueblo* AGER-2, ex-AKL-44, ex-FS-344, ex-FP-344, in the Philippines as a harbor craft beginning in July 1944. For the next decade the Coast-Guard-manned freight and supply (FS) ship served the Army, but was laid up in reserve in 1954 at Suisun Bay, California. Her career had been nondescript and uneventful.

In late 1965 and early 1966, a selection board of naval officers made a tour of the AKLs in the reserve fleet and selected the AKL-44 (*Pueblo*) and the AKL-45 (to become the U.S.S. *Palm Beach* AGER-3) as the most suitable candidates for conversion to intelligence gatherers. The criteria was simple: "inexpensive to convert and operate." Initially, the ships were to have been crewed with civilians, but salary costs were too high for the intended budget, so less expensive labor was sought. Naval personnel were ideal. Neither of the two AKLs was in prime condition, yet there was some life left. The *Pueblo* became a naval ship on April 12, 1966.

Both were taken to the Puget Sound Naval Shipyard in Bremerton, Washington, where top secret electronic equipment was installed for gathering and interpreting radio, radar, and sonar transmissions. In particular, the Navy wanted to acquire the submerged signatures of various Soviet submarines as well as eavesdrop on the North Koreans. Conversion to an electronic intelligence-gathering ship, or ELINT, was time consuming, and Captain Bucher and his crew faced one delay and crisis after another.

Finally, after much argument and hard feelings among shipyard staff, the *Pueblo* set out for a preliminary shakedown cruise in late July 1967, 10 months behind schedule. She was soon brought back under tow due to a faulty steering gear. The steering gear designed and built by a now defunct elevator company proved very unreliable. In September 1967, she left the shipyard for San Diego and training. She entered San Diego Harbor on September 22, 1967, and commenced various exercises. A formal inspection reviewed her performance and even in light of the ship's unusual nature and her novice crew, she was graded as overall "good" and certified for duty.

By December 1967, the *Pueblo* arrived in Japan for assignment. Crossing the Pacific was a major accomplishment as she broke down many times. Her steering gear was the major culprit. Captain Bucher was also vitally concerned about the ship's ability to defend itself. The ship was to have had installed 20-millimeter heavy machine guns, but instead two 50-caliber guns were provided. Pedestal mounts were sited fore and aft, and the guns were to be stowed when not needed. When attached to their mounts, they were covered with a canvas cover. As it was unwritten but accepted policy to avoid antagonizing potential belligerents, Admiral Frank L. Johnson, Commander Naval Forces Japan, counseled Bucher to "keep his guns covered and pointed down, or better yet, stowed below deck." Bucher was anxious about these instructions and what amounted to very poor guidance from all levels of the Navy and civilian leadership.

In essence, he and his ship were to gather critical and sensitive data from an unsuspecting enemy, and if caught, depend on the reputation of the "stars and stripes" to ward off any attack. The lessons learned from the Tonkin Gulf Incidents (August 1964) when the destroyers U.S.S. *Maddox* DD-731 and U.S.S. *C. Turner Joy* DD-951 fought it out with North Vietnamese coastal forces, and the attack on another ELINT ship, the U.S.S. *Liberty* AGTR-5 by Israeli forces (1967) had been ignored. In less than four years, the U.S. Navy had been twice scorched by entering the backyards of hostile third world nations. One of the three AGERs, known as Auxiliary General Environmental Research ships, the U.S.S. *Palm Beach,* U.S.S. *Banner,* or the U.S.S. *Pueblo* was about to become the victim of another incident. Given the inconsistency of direction from the various elements in the Naval chain of command and vague promises of instant air and naval support in the event of an emergency, Captain Bucher had much to worry him.

Twelve Days on Patrol and Seizure by the North Korean Navy

The *Pueblo* left the naval station at Sasebo, Japan, at 6 A.M. on January 11, 1968.

Her destination was the coast of North Korea on a mission that would last a mere 12 days. On January 23, 1968, four North Korean Russian-built *P-4* torpedo boats, accompanied by two Russian-designed modified *SO-1* gunboats, attacked the *Pueblo* in international waters off Wonsan Harbor. Despite repeated calls for help to anyone who would listen (including the White House), the ship and 82 of her crew were captives by nightfall. One crewman, Fireman Duane D. Hodges, was killed during the attack. Assurances that Naval or U.S. Air Force aircraft would respond to any request for assistance were hollow promises. In the higher echelons of the Navy and the Defense Department, no one was really sure what to do, so indecision allowed North Korean piracy of a U.S. ship.

In order to seize the ship, the attackers surrounded the *Pueblo* and raked her with 25-millimeter machine gun and 37-millimeter cannon fire. The *Pueblo* was defenseless as her two 50-caliber guns were shrouded by frozen canvas and never unmasked. Cautiously, the North Koreans boarded the ship, and when they were certain that there would be no resistance, they looted the personal property of the crew and beat and kicked their new charges. During the entire incident, the attackers watched the sky and sea, but the feared U.S. retaliation never came.

The ship surrendered without a fight, was brought into Wonsan Harbor, and later examined in Chong-gin by the Soviets. Their technicians were particularly interested in the antennas and other electronic equipment. Most of the classified material that had not been destroyed also fell into Russian hands. It was a rich harvest. The officer in charge of classified material, Lt. Stephen Harris, was unable to destroy much of the material as there was no destruct system. Again, the ship's designers had never envisioned an intelligence-gathering ship becoming an intelligence provider.

For the next 11 months Bucher, his officers, and crew suffered the tortures of the damned. They were put through intolerable strain and physical punishment. They all behaved like fighting men and committed no act to make the Navy or the country ashamed of them. On December 23, 1968, the 82 survivors were handed over to U.S. authorities after the United States signed a document that apologized for alleged spying and promised no reoccurrence of such an incident. The document was later repudiated.

By Christmas 1968 all were home in the United States as well as the remains of Fireman Hodges. For many it was over, but for some closure remains elusive. Commander Bucher and the crew were subsequently questioned in a formal court of inquiry as to the loss of a U.S. ship. After extensive testimony, the board of inquiry recommended that Bucher be bound over for General Court-Martial for surrendering his ship without resistance, among other charges. The *Pueblo's* executive officer, Lt. Edward Murphy, was to receive a letter of admonition, and Lt. Stephen Harris, the communications specialist, was also to be court-martialed. To these officers and many others, it was unbelievable! The court-martials never took place due to the intervention of the secretary of the Navy. In an act of political clemency, Secretary of the Navy John Chaffee dropped all charges. He simply stated, "They have suffered enough."

Epilogue

Lloyd Bucher faced a new dilemma. On one hand, he was considered a bona fide hero for saving the lives of his men. His devotion to them was and is unquestioned. On the other hand, the traditional naval establishment was abashed that he had allowed his ship to be seized without firing a shot. One senior officer put it in perspective when he declared, "At least one shot should have been fired in defense of the ship, just one shot would have been enough." Throughout the rest of his career, which was to last until June 1973, Bucher was regarded with some suspicion. He eventually secured an assignment on the staff of a Mine Force Flotilla and was involved in the mining of Haiphong Harbor in North Vietnam in April 1972. After this project, he began to actively consider retirement, which he did just over a year later.

After leaving the Navy, Bucher attempted a novel-writing career. His book, *Bucher: My Story*, published by Doubleday, was moderately successful and the publisher was anxious for another offering. He tried writing a humorous fictional account of submarine operations, but in his own words, "Writing was not for me." The publisher's advance was returned, and shortly thereafter he found his niche as a watercolor artist. He and his wife, Rose, reside in the San Diego area and his artwork is considered exceptional.

Bucher's executive officer, Lt. Edward Murphy, left the Navy soon after the incident and now sells recreational vehicles (RVs) in the San Diego area. Lt. Stephen Harris was promoted to Lt. Commander shortly after the court of inquiry and later left the Navy. He now teaches school in the Los Angeles area. Lt. (jg) Tim Harris, formerly the *Pueblo's* operations officer, was caught in the Iraqi invasion of Kuwait in August 1990. He barely escaped capture and thus avoided painful déjà vu. Lt. (jg) Skip Schumacher, a shining star of the *Pueblo's* crew, was offered a mediocre assignment after the board of inquiry announced its findings. Although he had not been charged or found lacking, he was still tainted by the "*Pueblo* Incident." He opted for resignation, and today looks back over a very successful career in banking in the St. Louis area. But what of the *Pueblo*?

In all probability, the North Koreans seized the ship because their Navy suspected she was a South Korean ship. Six of her class of light cargo ships had been part of the ROK fleet for years prior to the incident. The North Koreans had dispatched a patrol boat just 12 hours before the attack to photograph the *Pueblo* and a cursory comparison to like ships in the ROK Navy was made. Still smarting over their failed attempt to assassinate the South Korean president just days before, the spy ship was a natural target for retribution. Once they had her, and with no U.S. retaliation imminent, the American crew became an ideal means for embarrassing the United States. For internal distribution, the North Korean press published photos of the heavy cruiser U.S.S. *St. Paul* CA-73, identified as the *Pueblo*. For the North Koreans it was a national and international public relations coup.

The U.S.S. *Pueblo* AGER-2 is still carried on the U.S. Navy register as an active fleet unit. The North Koreans think otherwise and have turned her into a tourist attraction/museum in Wonsan Harbor. She has been remarkably well preserved and her current holder has no intention of returning the half-century-old ship to her rightful owners.

Dependent on the success of the three AGERs, the Navy was planning to have up to 30 of these ships roaming the seas. The pro-

A Soviet intelligence-gathering ship. These ships were common and dogged many U.S. warships and battle groups attempting to listen to ship-to-ship talk. *TIM*

gram was quietly canceled just after the *Pueblo*'s capture.

U.S.S. *Scorpion* SSN-589
Lost with All Hands, and Still a Mystery

There were two keels laid for the nuclear attack submarine *Scorpion* SSN-589. On November 1, 1957, the latest in the new *Skipjack*-class nuclear attack submarines was laid down at Electric Boat Company in Groton, Connecticut. Work proceeded on schedule, yet it suddenly became imperative that the United States have submarine-launched, intercontinental-ballistic-missile capability. Accordingly, the uncompleted hull of the *Scorpion* was conscripted and modified to become the world's first ballistic missile submarine able to launch its missiles from underwater. The Polaris submarine was born when the first *Scorpion* hull

was split and a 130-foot section was added to house 16 Polaris missile tubes. This new hybrid was renamed the U.S.S. *George Washington* SSBN-598, which was launched on June 9, 1959, and became operational soon thereafter.

U.S.S. Scorpion *SSN-589: A Skipjack-Class Submarine*

The second *Scorpion* was laid down on August 20, 1958, at the Electric Boat Company facility; launched on December 19, 1959; and commissioned on July 29, 1960. The *Skipjack* class combined the high speed and endurance benefits of a nuclear propulsion plant with a high-speed hull design. Tested in the conventionally powered submarine, U.S.S. *Albacore* AGSS-569, the teardrop hull was proven to be more conducive to underwater speed than that of previous hull shapes. The six-boat *Skipjack* class was the fifth class of nuclear attack subma-

Launching day for the U.S.S. *Scorpion* SSN-589 on December 18, 1959. *USNI*

rine. At $40 million per unit, *Skipjack*s initiated the birth of super-costly construction, costing twice as much as previous boats.

The *Skipjack*s were characterized by diving planes mounted on the sail as opposed to the forward hull, with a single center-mounted quiet-running screw rather than the two screws common in earlier designs. The teardrop hull design resulted in a beam-to-length ratio of 7.8 to 1.0, compared to that of 10.7 to 1.0 on previous nuclear attack boats. A beam of 31 feet introduced some very interesting possibilities, not the least of which was the mounting of her torpedo battery laterally, allowing the bow area for electronics. The 251-foot, 9-inch-long hull of the *Skipjack* class was also characterized by an ability to recess or retract any protrusions on the hull for even greater speed. Her nuclear reactor/propulsion plant was brand-new. Designated the S5W, it became the standard for attack submarines. Her steam turbine drove the boat at speeds of 20-plus knots on the surface and over 30 knots submerged. Compared to previous nuclear boats, this was over 10 knots faster and revolutionary for a submarine. Soviet submarines of that period were considerably slower and more noisy than the *Skipjack* class, thus the U.S. Navy had surged forward in the nuclear submarine race. This class carried six 21-inch torpedo tubes for armament and a crew varying from 99 to 114.

Operational History of the *Scorpion*

The *Scorpion* put to sea shortly after commissioning and was assigned to Submarine Squadron 6, Division 6. For the next three years the boat participated in various exercises off the eastern seaboard of the United States and as a NATO unit. During this period it was also distinguished by setting an endurance record of 70 hours being completely sealed up. In June 1963, she entered the Charleston Naval Shipyard and introduced the yard to its first nuclear submarine overhaul. A cofferdam was built around an opening made in the submarine's hull to allow access to equipment being updated or repaired. The *Scorpion* remained in the yard until May 1964; she then resumed active duty and was based out of Norfolk, Virginia—her last base of operations. Periodically the boat would make

The *Scorpion* at sea a year after the new submarine was launched. Unlike previous submarine classes, the diving planes are located on the sail rather than the hull. *USNI*

patrols into the Mediterranean, and it was during one of these patrols that her captain and crew were cited for meritorious service. This was unusual for a service in which excellence was considered standard.

In February 1967, the *Scorpion* was again given an overhaul and her first refueling, this time at the Norfolk Naval Shipyard. The work continued until late October when her crew began refresher and type training. For the next few months, the newly reconditioned attack submarine tested new weapon systems and finally, on February 15, 1968, she departed for service with the 6th Fleet in the Mediterranean. The *Scorpion* was now under the command of Commander Francis Slattery, who had reported aboard on October 17, 1967. Up through early May 1968, the boat operated in the Mediterranean, carrying out various controlled and "free play" exercises. The boat was rated overall excellent, yet there were nagging reports of unfinished repairs aboard the boat. Her final port visit was in Naples, Italy, from April 20–28, 1968, and then she put to sea. Her final contact with a shore base occurred just hours before her presumed loss. On the night of May 16–17, 1968, she briefly surfaced just outside the breakwater near Rota, Spain, and transferred two men

117

Nuclear submarines undergo repair at the Norfolk Naval Shipyard. The *Scorpion* looked much like these while being overhauled in late 1967. Since the loss of the *Thresher* SSN-593 and *Scorpion*, repair and overhaul standards have been greatly improved. *Author's Collection*

and seven messages ashore via a boat that had come out to greet the submarine. On May 21, 1968, her final transmission indicated that she was steaming west and was about 50 miles south of the Azores. This was the last word heard from the *Scorpion*.

The Loss of the Scorpion

The *Scorpion* was en route to the Norfolk Naval Station and was under electronic silence instructions except in the case of an emergency. Her set operational speed was 18 knots. As was procedure, at speeds over 15 knots, the stern dive planes were in emergency status at zero angle, and the depth was to be controlled within 10 feet by the fairwater planes. Watertight doors would typically have been open to allow access for normal operational and working parties; the officer of the deck (OOD) would have been in the control room; and the tasks of the diving officer and chief of the watch were combined for one watch stander. Drills were conducted daily, and despite the fact that the boat was going home, the crew was not permitted to relax from crucial duties.

The *Scorpion* was highly rated in the subma-

rine community and had done very well during her tour with the 6th Fleet. Her training was up-to-date, and the vast majority of her crew were well-qualified submariners. The U.S.S. *Scorpion* had an above-average crew, was just out of an overhaul, and was performing well. There had been no personnel problems or outward psychiatric problems among the men that required treatment or comment, thus the probability of sabotage or mental instability were unlikely factors in the subsequent loss of the boat.

On May 22, 1968, at approximately 6:44 P.M., the boat was presumed lost. She descended to the bottom of the ocean at depths of over 10,000 feet, 8,000 feet over her crush depth. At 10,000 feet, the pressure on the hull would have exceeded 5,000 psi, far more than the boat could tolerate. The reason why will probably never be known. Initially, it was suspected that one of her torpedoes exploded in the hull, yet it is now more probable that a faulty valve in the trash ejector mechanism allowed accidental flooding. Strong evidence further suggests that the *Scorpion* was operating at or near periscope depth when the mechanism failed and caused sea water to enter the boat and flood the 69-ton battery bank. This in turn caused an explosion and progressive,

The U.S.S. *William H. Standley* DLG-32 served as the headquarters ship during the ocean search for the *Scorpion*. USNI

irreparable damage. In any event the boat was somehow opened to the sea, and the water came in at a rate beyond the capability of damage control to cope. There is only so much that damage-control methodology, engine power, diving planes, and ballasting can provide in such situations. Damage-control doctrine never anticipated the submarine exceeding its crush depth. Twelve officers and 87 enlisted men went down with the boat and left no evidence on the surface.

The Search for the Wreck

The Navy responded within days of the incident after the *Scorpion* was declared missing. On May 27, 1968, Vice Admiral A. P. Schade (Commander, Submarine Force, Atlantic) embarked on the U.S.S. *Pargo* SSN-650 for an initial, first hand search attempt at the last suspected position of the missing boat. Subsequently, an intensive search began with 27 aircraft flights per day, 18 destroyer types, 12 submarines, 5 submarine rescue vessels, an oceano-

119

The oceanographic research ship U.S.S. *Mizar* AGOR-11 located the remains of a sunken nuclear submarine 10,000 feet under the Atlantic and 400 miles southwest of the Azores. This ship was designed to find radioactivity on the ocean floor at great depths as well as other chemical deposits. *USNI*

graphic survey ship, and a fleet oiler looking over the lost boat's intended course for a possible surface contact. In the next stage of the operation, Admiral L. G. Bernard left on the U.S.S. *Standley* DLG-32 to assume command of the search that would continue for days. Spread out as far as 40 miles from her suspected track, the search teams declared that there was a better than 97 percent chance that the *Scorpion* was not anywhere on the surface. The only vessel found was a World War

II submarine (probably a German U-boat) that the *Pargo* located. This hulk had been overlooked in previous scans. In early June 1968, the search widened to include warships in normal transit across the Atlantic and the services of the French submarine *Requin* were also graciously accepted. It was all to no avail.

Interestingly, a Soviet bloc *Krupny*-class guided-missile destroyer and an *ECHO-II*-class submarine were known to be in the area of the

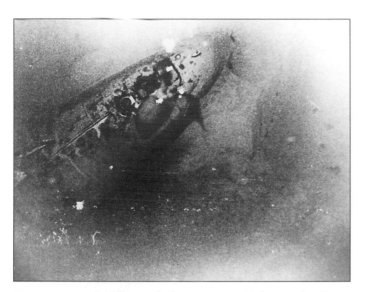

Bow section of the lost submarine at 10,000 feet under the ocean. The photographic equipment aboard the *Mizar* was remarkable to have captured this image taken on October 29, 1968. *USNI*

The aft hatch where the messenger buoy was stowed on the *Scorpion* as seen 10,000-plus feet beneath the Atlantic. The rope is still attached. Other items included two circular main ballast vents and two access hatches. *USNI*

A Soviet Navy *Krupny*-class guided missile destroyer. These were large, well-armed destroyers that mounted SSN-1 missiles, 16 57-millimeter guns and considerable ASW and antiship capability. One of these ships was seen in the vicinity of the last known position of the *Scorpion*. *TIM*

A Soviet *ECHO-II* submarine runs on the surface. One of this class was also seen near the disaster site, but the *Krupny*-class destroyer and this boat were exonerated of any accidental or deliberate attacks. *TIM*

A Soviet Navy supply ship known to service surveillance ships was near the area where the *Scorpion* was lost, but it too was found to be innocent of any wrongdoing. *USNI*

loss (within 200 miles of the *Scorpion*'s final estimated position). It was first thought that one of these units deliberately attacked and sank the *Scorpion,* however, a calculated or accidental attack by the Soviet Navy was eventually ruled out after all of the evidence was carefully analyzed.

On June 5, 1968, the chief of naval operations declared that the *Scorpion* was formally presumed lost. The secretary of the Navy also declared that all aboard the *Scorpion* were lost. The *Scorpion* was struck from the Navy list on June 30, 1968.

As the summer wore on, the search declined in strength, yet at the end of October 1968, the U.S.S. *Mizar* AGOR-11 located the remnants of a sunken nuclear submarine 400 miles southwest of the Azores. The *Mizar* utilized sensitive instruments that detect chemical and nuclear evidence on the ocean floor. The research ship detected parts of the *Scorpion* at 10,000 feet under the surface. With this find, the Navy sent the deep submersible *Trieste II* to investigate. Although the crew took photos and brought evidence to the surface, no conclusive finding has ever been made. The reason for the loss of the U.S.S. *Scorpion*, like so many others, will remain a mystery of the sea.

U.S.S. *Squalus* SS-192
Triumph in Submarine Rescue Operations

On May 23, 1939, the new attack submarine U.S.S. *Squalus* SS-192 made a "fast dive" test off the Isle of Shoals (near Portsmouth, New Hampshire) and failed to surface. Two days later, 33 of the 59-man crew were rescued from her forward compartments. The rescue was effected through the use of an innovative diving bell; however, 26 men were lost in the aft section of the submarine. This brought the total to 152 officers and men killed in the U.S. Navy's 37-year-old submarine service.

U.S.S. *Squalus:*
A Sargo-Class Submarine

The *Squalus* was laid down at the Portsmouth Navy Yard on October 18, 1937. She was one of five submarines of the *Sargo* class built over a two-year period from

The forward torpedo room of an "S" class, which resembled that of the *Squalus*. This was one of the compartments where 33 men huddled for hours waiting to be rescued. *Author's Collection*

The U.S.S. *Squalus* SS-192 shortly after being launched on September 14, 1938. *USNI*

The U.S.S. *Falcon* ASR-2, an early submarine rescue ship, situates herself over the wreck site based on information and markers the submarine *Sculpin* provided. *TIM*

A diver prepares to go over the side of the *Falcon* and down to the *Squalus* 240 feet below the surface. *TIM*

1938–1939. With an 11,000-mile range at 10 knots, these were long-legged submarines capable of extended patrols. Their design further signified preparations for a war with Imperial Japan. The *Squalus* displaced 1,450 tons, was 302 feet in length, and had a beam of 27 feet. Her three diesel engines could drive her at 20 knots (5,500 shaft horsepower) on the surface and her electric power plant could produce up to 8 knots (2,740 shaft horsepower) submerged. The *Sargo* class was air conditioned and had sufficient battery power for 2 knots over a 48-hour period. The boat was armed with eight 21-inch torpedo tubes, a 3-inch/50-caliber deck gun, and portable machine guns for surface defense.

The *Squalus* was launched on September 14, 1938, and commissioned on March 1, 1939, under the command of Lt. Oliver F. Naquin, an Annapolis graduate and expert in submarine operations. During March, April, and into late May 1939, the new submarine went through a series of tests and exercises to work out any builder deficiencies and acquaint the crew with this class. She carried a crew of 5 officers and 51 enlisted men when she departed Portsmouth on May 23, 1939, for a series of test dives that included fast or emergency procedures. She was also carrying two civilian Navy yard technicians and a company representative from the Winston Diesel Company, the manufacturer of the main propulsion plant.

The Loss of the Squalus

On May 23 at 7:30 A.M., the *Squalus* left the Portsmouth Navy Yard for a series of test dives that would include a "fast" descent procedure. The area selected for the exercises was just 5 miles off the Isle of Shoals and approximately 12 miles from the mainland. The depth of the water varied from 200 to 300 feet, and the sea bottom was described as blue mud. At 8:40 A.M., the submarine radioed the base that she would be diving for a period of one hour and would communicate again when surfaced. Two hours passed with no verification that the submarine had surfaced, so the base began radioing the submarine. By 11:30 A.M., it was obvious that the *Squalus* was not responding to repeated contacts; consequently, sister ship U.S.S. *Sculpin* SS-191 was sent to investigate. Two hours later the *Sculpin* was at or near the last known position of the *Squalus*, and a lookout sighted a smoke bomb in the water. The *Sculpin* maneuvered to the source of the smoke and found a 4-foot-long, yellow-painted cylinder which signified that a submarine was in difficulty and could not surface. "*SQUALUS*" was the name on the cylinder, which was attached by line to the submarine below. The cylinder also contained a telephone that was linked to the sunken boat. Contact was made at once with Lt. Naquin who indicated that the main induction valve had been open, allowing water to flood both forward and aft engine rooms as well as the aft torpedo room. This was sufficient to sink the

A scene from the film *Submarine D-1,* which starred Pat O'Brien. The film paralleled the tragedy of the *Squalus* with two major exceptions. The fictional "D-1" was sunk by ramming, and nearly all of the crew were saved. *TIM*

boat and she was on the bottom. He suggested that the best way to save the crew and boat was to have divers close the valve and attach air lines to the boat to provide sufficient buoyancy to surface. He advised against the crew escaping by using the *Momsen* breathing lungs due to the 240-foot depth and the probability of "bends." Submarine crews received escape training using the lung, but at no more than a 120-foot depth.

Lt. Naquin attempted to continue with his report, but the cable attached to the marker buoy separated and communication was cut off. The *Sculpin* immediately anchored over the *Squalus* and radioed the base for assistance.

Aboard the *Squalus* 33 men were alive in the forward compartments; however, the 26 men who were in the aft compartments perished by the time the boat hit the bottom stern first. Luckily, five men from the aft part of the boat just made it into the control room as water rushed upward, Electrician's Mate Lloyd Maness dogged the hatch shut just in time to prevent the entire boat from being flooded. As the boat slid downward, the crew made attempts to surface by blowing the forward

ballast tanks, but to no avail. The men released the forward marker buoy in the hope that a passing boat or aircraft would investigate. The 33 men, including the commanding officer, began to assess their situation. There was sufficient air for up to 72 hours, including that stored in flasks for emergencies. Food consisted of emergency rations and various canned items, and lighting came from individual flashlights and lamps. Aside from the fear of being confined in what probably would become their coffin, the cold was intense. The water temperature at 240 feet was 31 degrees Fahrenheit, causing the interior of the forward compartment to reach 36 degrees. Blankets were available and the men sat close together, but the outlook was dismal. Periodically, the crew hammered Morse code messages on the hull in the hope that someone somewhere would hear.

At 9:45 P.M., the oscillograph (a sound-detection system) aboard the *Sculpin* heard Lt. Naquin's signal, "Conditions satisfactory, but cold." Ashore, the Navy summoned every diver available and ordered the rescue vessel U.S.S. *Falcon* ASR-2 and the new light cruiser

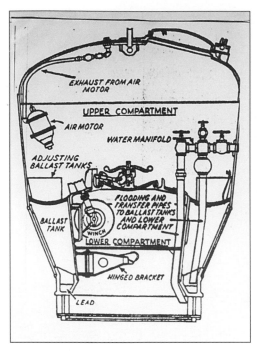

A cutaway drawing of the diving bell. Essentially the bell, connected with cables and air hoses to the mother ship, was released to float to the sunken submarine. Once there, air pressure equalized with the submarine as the bell was attached to a prefitted escape hatch. The chamber door was opened and survivors allowed to board. Then the bell ascended and repeated the procedure until all survivors were saved. *TIM*

U.S.S. *Brooklyn* CL-40 to the scene. By 5:30 A.M. on May 24, 1939, the *Falcon* was at the site as well as other smaller rescue ships. The *Brooklyn* arrived later with 3,000 feet of air hose and was ordered to fulfill the unenviable role as a floating media base.

One of the Most Amazing Rescues in U.S. Naval History

The *Falcon* was transporting an innovative and never before used diving bell, or escape chamber. The loss of the submarine *S-4* and her 40-man crew in December 1927 inspired the development of this rescue chamber. A team of specialists led by Commander Allen McCann designed and built it in 1930. The thick steel chamber weighed 18,000 pounds and was bell- or pear-shaped. In essence it was an unpowered minisubmarine and operated similar to the present-day DSRV (deep submergence rescue vehicle). The bell

was divided into a large upper compartment and a small lower compartment. The sealed upper compartment carried a three-man crew and the lower compartment was open to the sea with a large rubber seal that encased the circular base of the bell.

The process began with a diver being lowered over the side of the rescue vessel to descend to the submarine in distress. He would attempt to connect a steel cable from the base of the bell to one of the eye bolts near the boat's escape hatch. When this was accomplished, the bell could be lowered and follow the line down to the submarine. Next, the bell was lowered by the rescue ship's boom, submerged into the sea until it reached the submarine, where it was attached to the hull. After the water in the small lower compartment was removed, the upper compartment hatch in the chamber was opened as was the submarine escape hatch, and a maximum of eight men could escape into the upper chamber. The bell was then brought to the surface, unloaded, and then returned to the submarine for more survivors. The process would be repeated until all were saved—that was the theory at least.

The *Falcon* was moored securely to the sea floor by 10 A.M. on May 24 and the rescue operation was now under the overall command of Admiral C. W. Cole. By 10:15 A.M., a hard hat diver, Boatswains Mate 2nd class Martin Siblitzky, was on his way to the *Squalus*. Diving to a depth of 240 feet was made easier for him by breathing a mixture of helium and oxygen. The diver followed the grappling line to the bottom and at 10:22 A.M., the diver touched the deck of the downed submarine and began to grope for the forward escape hatch. The water pressure at 240 feet is 105.6 pounds per square inch, and although the diver could loiter for over an hour below, he could exert himself for no more than 20 minutes. Twenty minutes was all the time available to attach the downhaul cable from the lower compartment of the rescue bell to the submarine's escape hatch. Just at the limit of his time, the diver was able to hook the downhaul to the eye bolt of the forward hatch. He then ascended to the surface.

At 11:40 A.M., the diving bell was lowered into the water with its three-man crew and began a slow descent following the attached downhaul line. The bell settled on the hull and the rubber seal was secured to the escape hatch.

A view of a diving bell or chamber on the deck of the rescue ship U.S.S. *Mallard* ASR-4 in February 1942. It had been rushed to where the submarine *S-26* had gone down in 301 feet of water. Unfortunately, the docking system was not compatible, and the crew could not be rescued. *TIM*

The eye rings that surround the hatch of the U.S.S. *Pampanito* SS-383. This is similar to that aboard the *Squalus*, and not much changed on later boats such as the nuclear-powered *Scorpion* and *Thresher. Author's Collection by David Lanzaro*

A view of the escape hatch below deck of the *Pampanito*. The diving bell or DSRV (deep submergence rescue vehicle) attached itself to this area on deck and equalized air pressure with the submarine before popping the hatches. *Author's Collection by David Lanzaro*

Squalus survivors pour out of the diving chamber onto the deck of the rescue ship *Falcon* on the afternoon of May 24, 1939. *TIM*

The light cruiser *Brooklyn* sped to the disaster site from New York City where the 1939 World's Fair was being held. She left so quickly that a few of her crew did not make it back aboard in time for sailing. *TIM*

Inflatable pontoons used to lift the sunken submarine to the surface during salvage efforts. *TIM*

Pontoons are connected to the *Squalus* and then inflated to bring the sunken boat to the surface. *TIM*

On September 13, 1939, the *Squalus* broke the surface and was towed into Portsmouth for an overhaul and upgrade. *TIM*

The sea-growth-encrusted submarine sits in dry dock at the Portsmouth Navy Yard in preparation for a full overhaul. *USNI*

Recommissioned as the *Sailfish* on May 15, 1940, a year after she sank, the former *Squalus* went on to an illustrious career in the Pacific War. Her conning tower is currently located on the grounds of the Naval base at Portsmouth. *USNI*

Air pressure was adjusted, and the escape hatch to the *Squalus* was opened. Thirty-three cold but grateful men looked at their rescuers. Seven men were selected based on their physical and emotional condition and were transported to the surface. They boarded the *Falcon* at 1:20 P.M. after being trapped below for over 28 hours.

The bell immediately descended for the next group and at 4 P.M. it broke the surface with nine more men. Thirty minutes later, the bell began its next descent, and returned at 6:50 P.M. with nine more survivors. Only two crew of the bell were being sent down instead of three to allow as much room as possible for survivors. At 8:51 P.M., the crew of the bell reported that they had the last eight men from the forward compartment, and the bell was hovering at 90 feet above the wreck site. The last survivors, Lt.

Naquin, his executive officer, and six crew were on their way to the surface when the bell's down-haul cable jammed. What had been a letter-perfect rescue for the untried diving bell was interrupted for three hours while a diver unjammed the downhaul. Finally, at 38 minutes after midnight on May 25, the bell surfaced next to the *Falcon*. For Naquin and the other seven men, it had been nearly 40 hours of fear and anticipation. It was accepted that the 26 men in the aft compartments of the *Squalus* were dead, yet the bell was later lowered to verify this. When it was attached to the aft escape hatch and the hatch opened, only water surging from the interior of the downed submarine greeted them. The rescue effort was then ceased, and families of the lost men notified. Local hospitals treated and released the survivors. The air in the *Squalus* was extremely foul at the end and, had the rescue effort been a few hours later, it was doubtful that 33 men could have been saved. The diving bell was an unqualified success, and the rescue effort a tribute to the courage and devotion to duty of the divers and bell operators.

Salvage of the Squalus and Probable Reason for the Sinking

The probable reason that the submarine sank was that her main air induction valve was stuck in its open position at the beginning of the boat's 18th test dive. This valve is 31 inches in diameter and located near the conning tower. As the submarine began its dive, the valve and its subsidiary valves were to close automatically as the boat propulsion plant converted to electric power. A light on the control board indicated that it was closed. A mechanical malfunction left it open, and by the time the alarm was sounded, the boat was doomed.

The *Squalus* was raised to the surface on September 13, 1939, and towed to the Portsmouth Navy Yard for reconditioning. The salvage was long and arduous for the divers who with great difficulty attached cables to the hull and inflatable pontoons. The submarine was recommissioned on May 15, 1940, as the U.S.S. *Sailfish* SS-192. She went to the Pacific War and ultimately earned nine battle stars and a Presidential Unit Citation. Shortly after the end of World War II, the now obsolete boat was scrapped. The May 1939 loss of 26 men in the *Squalus* sinking was a great naval tragedy; however, the rescue of 33 men was a triumph for Navy divers.

U.S.S. *Thresher* SSN-593
Untimely Death of a Shark

At 9:17 A.M. on April 10, 1963, a radio operator aboard the U.S.S. *Skylark* ARS-20 (a submarine rescue ship) routinely was monitoring transmissions from the U.S.S. *Thresher* SSN-593. He heard what he thought was, "We're past the trial depth," followed by a tremendous roaring noise and then a deathly silence. Moments earlier he had heard the all-too-familiar sound of pressurized air being forced into ballast tanks, yet he could not imagine that the nuclear-powered attack submarine *Thresher* was in mortal danger and had less than four minutes to live. Frantic calls to the submarine produced the same result—silence. Hours later, any hope of the submarine and her crew of 108 officers and men, as well as 4 naval officers (observers) and 17 civilian technicians being rescued faded. Vintage nuclear submarines from the 1960s could not survive at depths beyond 2,000 feet. The fathometer registered 8,400 feet in this area of the sea. Apparently the *Thresher*, the most modern and advanced of the U.S. Navy's growing arsenal of nuclear attack boats, had imploded somewhere beyond her maximum diving depth.

U.S.S. Thresher SSN-593: The Very Best in the U.S. Navy

The U.S.S. *Thresher* was launched and commissioned at the Portsmouth Navy Yard on July 9, 1960. She was the lead boat of a class of attack submarines that would number 14 units and operate worldwide. Since the original design for the U.S.S. *Nautilus* SSN-571 was inaugurated in 1951, the Navy built a series of seven designs before settling on the *Thresher*, which was the eighth class of nuclear submarines in as many years. Not since the World War I era of successive battleship designs had such a phenomenon occurred in U.S. naval construction. Once nuclear power was made safely available to submersibles, technology advanced so quickly as to force one improved design after another.

The *Thresher* class displaced 3,750 tons on the surface and 4,470 tons submerged. These boats were 278.5 feet in length with a beam of 31.7 feet and drew 28.4 feet. The nuclear-powered *Thresher* was similar to the *Skipjack*, but was of a modified teardrop construction. She carried four torpedo tubes amidships, two to port and two to starboard, all angled 10

The new nuclear submarine U.S.S. *Thresher* SSN-593 at speed shortly after being launched. *TIM*

degrees from the centerline. Her fire-control computer, the first digital system installed on a submarine, was selected for its ability to fire the Navy's SUBROC ASW weapon, then in development.

The *Thresher* was capable of 18-plus knots on the surface and 30-plus knots submerged, made possible by a single Westinghouse S5W pressurized, water-cooled nuclear reactor. The reactor provided steam to two sets of geared turbines that delivered 15,000 horsepower to a single shaft and propeller. Her operating depth was 1,300-plus feet, with a maximum depth of just under 2,000 feet. The normal cruise complement was 114 officers and men. On August 3, 1961, her commission pennant was raised.

The new boat embarked on a series of mandatory and programmed trials designed to iron out any problems and acclimate her crew to their new surroundings. Her crew was well-trained technically, yet it was necessary for them to cooperatively interact for the submarine to be a success. This was certainly the case as the new submarine became a part of the fleet.

For the first year after commissioning, the new boat was held under a microscope. The immediate future of the attack submarine fleet was riding on her performance, and perform she did. Her sonar proved more impressive than anticipated and the test firing of various torpedoes was deemed a success. She was quieter and faster than anything underwater, and when subjected to massive depth charge attacks (including a severe shock test), she bore up well.

The *Thresher* pushed submarine warfare to a new threshold. Congress was so excited by this new submarine it ultimately funded the construction of 13 more boats, plus an 11-boat follow-on class (*Sturgeon*). The only incident that marred an otherwise positive inaugural year was when a Port Canaveral tug struck her and damaged a ballast tank. She left Florida for the Electric Boat facility in Groton, Connecticut, and was repaired quickly enough to complete exercises and testing. On July 16, 1962, she arrived in the Portsmouth Navy Yard at Kittery, Maine, for a six-month period of overhaul.

A Roaring Noise, Then Silence: The Loss of the Thresher

Thresher's overhaul was planned for six months; however, this was extended for an additional two and a half months. As with any organization that employs high-tech machin-

133

The classic pose of a Cold War nuclear submarine—nuclear attack boat *Thresher* slowly moves through the water. Her diving planes are sited on her sail, and her hull numbers and draft marks are easily seen. On September 6, 1963, another view of her hull number will forever haunt the Navy and the American public. It was seen on a large piece of her hull that was discovered 8,400 feet under the Atlantic, five months after her loss. *TIM*

ery, when a piece of equipment is shut down for repair, it is only natural to make improvements and take advantage of any known and applicable technological advancements. So it was with the *Thresher*. In her case, she was retained to decrease her noise signature. On April 4, 1963, the refitted boat entered dry dock for final work and a check to ensure that all fittings were secure. The importance of ensuring that all fittings are secure was later graphically demonstrated with the sinking of the U.S.S. *Guitarro* SSN-665. On May 16, 1969, at the Mare Island Navy Yard in Vallejo, California, the *Guitarro* was found on the bot-

tom of the harbor next to her fitting-out pier. Loose fittings and hoses allowed the submarine to sink, much to the embarrassment of yard personnel.

On April 8, 1963, the refurbished *Thresher* left the dry dock and was back in the water alongside a pier. Her crew and civilian yard workers and technicians were in each other's way as they clamored over one another inside.

The submarine was now under the command of Lt. Commander John W. Harvey. With 19 other officers (4 as observers), a crew of 92 men, and 17 civilian technicians, it was time to go to sea. The *Thresher* had been tested thoroughly in harbor. Her remaining tests, including deep diving, were to be conducted at sea before she could rejoin the fleet. At five minutes after 8 A.M. on April 9, 1963, the 278-foot-long submarine cast off and headed for open waters.

Joining the submarine three hours later was the U.S.S. *Skylark* ARS-20, a submarine rescue ship assigned to Submarine Squadron 10. The *Skylark* was one of three 1,235-ton fleet tugs built during and just after World War II that were subsequently converted for submarine rescue. In 1947, the *Skylark* underwent conversion and was equipped with specialized pumps, compressors, and a submarine rescue chamber. Her actual purpose was to provide a communications link to the submarine and ward off any unwelcome ships or craft in the operational area. She was ill equipped to assist a nuclear-powered submarine should it encounter major problems at any real depth, and there was no equipment available for rescue work. All she really could provide was a link to the surface.

At 11 A.M., the *Thresher* and her escort sailed for a destination off Boston where the submarine would begin a series of planned dives—in potentially salvageable waters. Throughout the day, the boat made progressively deeper dives as the crew and observers carefully watched fittings and all equipment for failure. The submarine dove in small increments of less than 100 feet, slowly allowing seawater into certain systems.

The *Thresher* bade the *Skylark* farewell late on April 9, after successfully completing the first element of her formal Sea Trial Agenda. The converted tug steamed into the distance with instructions to meet at a point 220 miles east of Cape Cod, where deep submergence tests would be made the following

The *Sturgeon*-class U.S.S. *Pintado* SSN-672 at the Alameda Naval Air Station during the 1996 San Francisco Navy Fleet Week. The outstanding performance of the *Thresher* helped to launch her and two dozen other vitally needed attack submarines. The escape hatch eye bolts are easily seen up forward. *Author's Collection*

day. At 6:35 A.M., the *Skylark* promptly hove into sight at the appointed location, yet the *Thresher* was not on the surface. The submerged submarine then provided her location and bearing and notified *Skylark* that she was about to resume testing. The *Thresher* was so silent, that had it been wartime and the *Skylark* an enemy ship, she would have been torpedoed and on her way to the bottom without ever knowing of her assailant.

The depth of water under the *Skylark*'s keel was 8,400 feet. The *Thresher* began her descent to her planned test depth in increments, again with all crew and observers carefully monitoring her progress. As she slowly descended, it is surmised that one of her seawater connections began to leak, and as she reached the test dive depth, it became a visible and obvious danger to the crew. This must have been shortly after 9 A.M., as it was in a five-minute period from 9:12 A.M. to 9:17 A.M. that the problem escalated and got out of control. It is further suspected

that the leak occurred in the engine spaces, thus causing an interruption in propulsive power (reactor SCRAM). A violent and uncontrollable spray must have erupted from one of her sea connection pipes that shorted out critical electrical equipment and quickly flooded the compartment beyond hope of recovery. The boat, now without power, could no longer maneuver and was at the mercy of progressive flooding. Growing pressure against the hull by a rapidly increasing depth ensured an inevitable end. Shortly after the *Thresher* passed her last possible safe depth, implosion disintegrated her hull. On the surface, anxiety grew with each passing moment. Against a noise background probably generated by blowing ballast tanks, a garbled message was received by the lone rescue ship indicating difficulties at her test depth. Immediately thereafter there was roaring noise followed by silence.

At first, anxiety was tempered by recounting past experiences of garbled messages and

The destroyer leader U.S.S. *Norfolk* DL-1, used in the early stages of the search for the sunken submarine. *TIM - SFCB*

sounds of forced air. Thermal layers at different depths and surface disturbances could account for the distorted message, and the operator aboard the *Thresher* had further indicated that she was attempting to seek a shallower depth or the surface to correct her immediate problems. A message was quickly sent to the submarine that the surface was clear of shipping and any obstructions and to surface as they were able. Finally, a decision had to be made. Emergency signals were begun and a systematic surface search initiated. This produced no result and, regrettably, the *Skylark* had to inform the shore establishment that the *Thresher* was missing. Shortly after noon, the message that the submarine had failed to surface or respond to any emergency signals was on its way up the Navy hierarchy. All forces available in the area were ordered to converge on the *Skylark*, still standing a lonely vigil.

By 6:30 P.M. on April 10, 1963, 15 major

ships were en route to the *Skylark*'s position. These included the destroyer leader U.S.S. *Norfolk* DL-1, destroyer U.S.S. *Blandy* DD-943, submarine rescue ship U.S.S. *Recovery* ARS-43, and the research vessel *Atlantis II* from the Woods Hole Oceanographic Institute. Before most of the ships arrived, the *Recovery* located and marked a definite oil slick in the immediate vicinity of the disaster. The *Skylark* discovered several cork pieces and a tube of cooking flavor, and the U.S.S. *Sunbird* ARS-15 picked up rubber gloves as did the destroyer U.S.S. *Warrington* DD-843. The civilian ship *Atlantis II* tested water samples in the vicinity and her analysts declared that there was no adverse radioactivity from the reactor, presumably one and a half miles under the surface.

Task Group 89.7, under the command of Rear Admiral Lawson P. Ramage, assumed control of the search operation for the next few days. The search was then reassigned to Captain Frank

The starboard side of the *Thresher* plainly shows her hull number. The crew aboard the bathyscaph *Trieste* took this photograph during an early September 1963 dive. *TIM - SFCB*

Andrews, commander of the *Thresher's* Squadron. Andrews temporarily established his base of operations on the *Warrington*, and for the next several months, ships used advanced fathometer equipment and other highly refined electronic search devices. During this second phase of the search, this group at one time or another included 28 warships and 5 dedicated ocean research units. Often the sole on-site units were the civilian-manned *Atlantis II* or the U.S.N.S. *Conrad* AGOR-3. It was not until the Navy's premier underwater search vehicle, the bathyscaph *Trieste*, was brought from the West Coast to the region off Cape Cod that the search entered a new and more productive phase.

The Bathyscaphe Trieste and the Search Ends

The bathyscaph *Trieste* had been purchased from the French who had pioneered the concept of deep-diving submersibles. The *Trieste* had already descended to 36,000 feet in the Marianas Trench two years before, so 8,400 feet would present no problem. The submersible arrived on the scene on June 21,

The *Trieste*, in the foreground, prepares for its initial dive on the wreck site in late June 1963. A submarine rescue ship, the U.S.S. *Preserver* ARS-8, is on station in the background. *TIM*

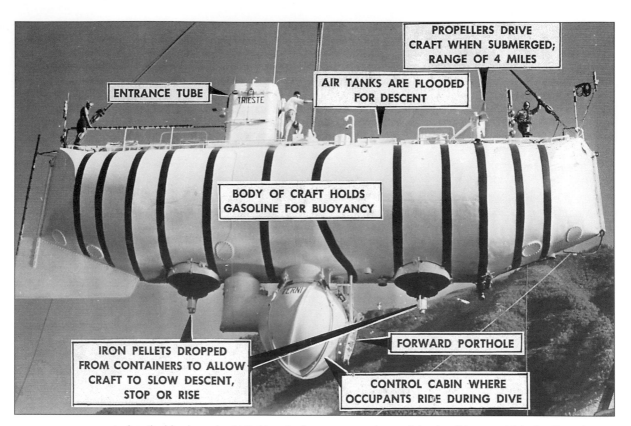

PROPELLERS DRIVE
CRAFT WHEN SUBMERGED;
RANGE OF 4 MILES

ENTRANCE TUBE

AIR TANKS ARE FLOODED
FOR DESCENT

BODY OF CRAFT HOLDS
GASOLINE FOR BUOYANCY

IRON PELLETS DROPPED
FROM CONTAINERS TO ALLOW
CRAFT TO SLOW DESCENT,
STOP OR RISE

FORWARD PORTHOLE

CONTROL CABIN WHERE
OCCUPANTS RIDE DURING DIVE

A detailed look at the U.S. Navy's deep-water submersible the *Trieste*, which the French developed and the Navy purchased. *TIM - SFCB*

1963, and over the next several weeks, made a series of 10 dives to various selected sites on the ocean floor.

During her final series of dives, the *Trieste* located and successfully filmed a large and definite piece of the *Thresher* on September 6. A part of her hull showing her draft marks and her number "593" was enough. It was over, and on September 7, 1963, the search was officially ended. It was clear that the implosion had spread the submarine over a very large area of the ocean bottom, and further expense and search was useless.

A formal Navy court of inquiry absolved any of the *Thresher*'s officers and men of any blame for the incident and recommended a number of changes in how pipes, fittings, and other potentially unreliable pieces of equipment should be examined and tested in the future. The legacy of *Thresher* and her crew was simple: Do the best that is humanly possible to ensure that naval ships are accident-proof. Over the last three decades, that legacy has resulted in improved safety in submarine operations. The *Thresher* may have suffered an untimely death, but she will always be remembered.

BIBLIOGRAPHY

Primary Materials

Private Papers—Manuscript/Photo Files
  Bonner, Kermit H. Jr.—various.
  Tacey, Steven—S.S. *America.*

Special Collections—Manuscript/Photo Collections
  Call Bulletin Newspaper Photo File, 1994, Treasure
    Island Museum—various.
  Navy League of the United States, 1998—U.S.S. *Iowa,*
    U.S.S. *Enterprise.*
  San Francisco Maritime Museum, 1998—U.S.S.
    Benevolence.
  Treasure Island Museum Photo Files, 1994—various.
  United States Naval Institute, 1997, 1998—various.

Interviews
  Bonner, Kermit H. Sr., Lt. Commander, USN, Ret., life
    aboard a plane guard destroyer.
  Bucher, Lloyd, Commander USN, Ret., loss of the
    U.S.S. *Pueblo.*
  Burgess, Rick, fire on board the U.S.S. *Enterprise.*
  Daniel, John E., U.S.S. *West Point.*
  Hall, Eva, fire aboard the U.S.S. *Oriskany.*
  Hunter, L. L., explosion in turret 2, U.S.S. *Mississippi.*
  Killmeyer, Kenneth, fire aboard the U.S.S. *Forrestal.*
  Naval Attaché, Embassy of North Korea, Washington, D.C.
  Newly, W., fire aboard the U.S.S. *Enterprise.*
  Ritchie, W., U.S.S. *Iowa.*
  Santiago, Reynaldo, fire aboard the U.S.S. *Oriskany.*
  Shanaberger, R., U.S.S. *Turner.*
  Stillwell, Paul, U.S.S. *Mississippi,* U.S.S. *Missouri.*
  Swanson, Robert, fire aboard the U.S.S. *Oriskany.*

U.S. Government Documents
  Basic Military Requirements, Naval Educational and
    Training Command, 1986.
  Judge Advocate General, USN, "Loss of the Scorpion,"
    confidential report, 1969.

Secondary Materials

Books, Monographs, Treaties
  Alden, John D. *The American Steel Navy.* Naval Institute
    Press, 1972.
  Beach, Edward L. *The Wreck of the Memphis.* Holt,
    Rinehart & Winston, 1966.
  Beigel, Harvey M. *Battleship Country.* Pictorial Histories
    Publishing, 1983.
  Blackman, Raymond, ed. *Jane's Fighting Ships,
    1968–1969.* Jane's Publishing Group, 1970.
  Bonner, Kit. *Final Voyages.* Turner Publishing, 1996.
  Bucher, Lloyd. *Bucher: My Story.* Doubleday &
    Company, 1970.
  Chant, Christopher. *Sea Forces of the World.* Crescent
    Books, 1990.

Chesneau, Roger. *The World's Aircraft Carriers, 1914–1945*. Arms and Armour Press, 1986.

Delgado, James, and Stephen Haller. *Shipwrecks at the Golden Gate*. Lexicos, 1989.

Dulin, Robert, and William Garzke. *Battleships*. Naval Institute Press, 1976.

First Shot Naval Veterans, *U.S.S.* Ward *DD-139*. Naval Veterans Company, 1986.

Friedman, Norman. *U.S. Cruisers*. Naval Institute Press, 1984.

Friedman, Norman. *Carrier Air Power*. Naval Institute Press, 1981.

Friedman, Norman. *U.S. Destroyers*. Naval Institute Press, 1982.

Friedman, Norman. *U.S. Naval Weapons*. Naval Institute Press, 1985.

Gibbs, James A. *Shipwrecks of the Pacific Coast*. Binford and Mort Publishing, 1957.

Gibbs, James. *Peril at Sea*. Schiffer Publishing, 1986.

Hillman, Raymond. *The Loss of the Navy Cruiser U.S.S. Milwaukee*. Pride of the River, 1994.

Hudson, Kenneth, and Ann Nicholls. *Tragedy on the High Seas*. A & W Publishers, 1979.

Humble, Richard. *Submarines, The Illustrated History*. Basinghall Books Limited, 1981.

Lockwood and Adamson. *Tragedy at Honda*. Doubleday, 1960.

Miller, Nathan. *The U.S. Navy, An Illustrated History*. American Heritage Publishing, 1977.

Moeser, Robert D. *U.S. Navy: Vietnam*. Naval Institute Press, 1969.

Moore, J. E., ed. *Jane's Fighting Ships, 1986–1987*. Jane's Publishing Company, 1987.

Moore, John R., Captain RN. *The Soviet Navy Today*. Stein and Day, 1975.

Morison, Samuel Elliott. *History of United States Naval Operations in World War II*, all volumes. Atlantic Little Brown & Company, 1962.

Morris, Douglas. *Cruisers of the Royal and Commonwealth Navies*. Maritime Books, 1987.

Morris, James M. *History of the U.S. Navy*. Brompton Books, 1993.

Office of Naval History. *U.S. Navy, Dictionary of American Naval Fighting Ship*s, all volumes. U.S. Government Printing Office, 1969–1975.

Preston, Anthony. *Aircraft Carriers*. Brompton Books, 1979.

Preston, Anthony. *Battleships*. Gallery Books, 1979.

Quinn, William P. *Shipwrecks Along the Atlantic Coast*. Parnassus Imprints, 1988.

Reilly, John. *United States Navy Destroyers of World War II*. Blandford Press, 1983.

Silverstone, Paul H. *U.S. Warships Since 1945*. Naval Institute Press, 1987.

Stillwell, Paul. *Battleship Missouri, An Illustrated History*. Naval Institute Press, 1996.

Swaney, Edwin S. *Operation Crossroads*. Sutherland Publishing, 1986.

Sweetman, Jack. *American Naval History*. Naval Institute Press, 1984.

Tazewell, William. *Newport News Shipbuilding—The First Century*. Mariners Museum, 1986.

Terzibaschitsch, Stefan. *Aircraft Carriers of the U.S. Navy*. Naval Institute Press, 1978.

Wingate, John, DSC. *Warships in Profile—Vol. II*. Doubleday and Company, 1973.

Articles

Bradley, Mark A. "Why They Called the *Scorpion* 'Scrapiron.' " Naval Institute *Proceedings,* July 1998.

Foster, Captain Wynn E. "Fire on the Hangar Deck." *The Hook*, Tailhook Association, Winter 1988.

Grenfell, E. W. "U.S.S. *Thresher*, 3 August 1961–April 1963." Naval Institute *Proceedings*, March 1964.

Nervig, C. A. "The *Cyclops* Mystery." Naval Institute *Proceedings*, January 1970.

Peniston, Robert C. "Battleships: Past, Present, and Future." Captain Naval Review, Naval Institute *Proceedings*, May 1990.

Powers, Robert C. "Proceed to Assist . . . The *Belknap* Disaster." Naval Institute *Proceedings*, August 1976.

Rigler, Capt. Frank V. "Navy Returning to Sunken Hulk Believed to be U.S.S. *Cyclops*." Naval Institute *Proceedings*, August 1973.

Steven, Mark, Loren Jekins, and Jeff Copeland. "Collision Course—U.S.S. *Belknap*." *Newsweek*, December 8, 1975.

Unpublished Works

U.S.S. *Mississippi* cruise book—1943/1944.

U.S.S. *Missouri* cruise book—1945.

World War II Memories, U.S.S. *Mississippi*.

Newspapers

Baldwin, Hanson W. "Sunken Submarine is of Latest Type." *New York Times*, May 24, 1939 [U.S.S. *Squalus* SS-192].

Benson, Bruce. "Just Like a Drill—With Too Much Realism." *Honolulu Advertiser*, January 16, 1969 [U.S.S. *Enterprise* CVAN-65].

Grutzner, Charles. "46 Killed, 7 Missing on Carrier Fire at Brooklyn Navy Yard, Workers Trapped Below Decks." *New York Times*, December 20, 1960 [U.S.S. *Constellation* CVA-64].

Grutzner, Charles. "Cavanaugh Scores Navy Yard as Lax in Fire on Carrier." *New York Times*, December 21, 1960 [U.S.S. *Constellation* CVA-64].

Grutzner, Charles. "Earlier Fires on Carrier Cited." *New York Times*, December 21, 1960 [U.S.S. *Constellation* CVA-64].

Lueras, Leonard. "'Big E' Casualties Recall Tragedy." *Honolulu Advertiser*, January 14, 1969 [U.S.S. *Enterprise* CVAN-65].

Lueras, Leonard. "Cause of Disaster Still Sought." *Honolulu Advertiser*, January 14, 1969 [U.S.S. *Enterprise* CVAN-65].

Mitchell, Wallace. "Navy Panel Starts 'Big E' Fire Probe." *Honolulu Advertiser*, January 17, 1969 [U.S.S. *Enterprise* CVAN-65].

Newton, Marshall. "Hope for 26 in *Squalus*; Opening of Hatch Reveals Water Filled Their Section." *New York Times*, May 24, 1939 [U.S.S. *Squalus* SS-192].

O'Conner, Hap. "Sadness Marks Navy Funeral." *Los Angeles Times*, June 17, 1924 [U.S.S. *Mississippi* BB-41].

Randall, Hon. Ellis R. "Captain Bacon's Role Told in Sinking of *Benevolence*." *Vallejo Independent Press*, September 3, 1980 [U.S.S. *Benevolence* AH-13].

Staff Writer. "Special Board to Investigate Disaster." *New York Times*, May 25, 1939 [U.S.S. *Squalus* SS-192].

Staff Writer. "18 Die, 487 Safe as Hospital Ship Sinks off Gate." *San Francisco Call Bulletin*, August 26, 1950 [U.S.S. *Benevolence* AH-13].

Swift, Earl. "The Gray Ghost." *Norfolk Compass*, September 24, 1989 [U.S.S. *West Point* AP-23].

Wheelwright, Ralph. "Witness Swears Hand of Victim Hit Control." *Los Angeles Times*, June 17, 1924 [U.S.S. *Mississippi* BB-41].

Web Sites

http://www.whrc.navy.mil: Arkin, William. "Fire on U.S. Warship in 1975 Reportedly Neared A-Weapons." 1989.

http://www.cvn65.navy.mil: "Big E Statistics." Big E Fun Facts site.

http://www.kennedy.navy.mil: "History of U.S.S. *John F. Kennedy*." Kennedy Home Page.

http://www.missouri.navy.mil: "U.S.S. Missouri." FAQ, Military USN site.

Other

Navy League. "Sea Power, 1994, 1996, 1997, 1998 Almanacs." Navy League of the United States.

Warner Brothers Film Company. *Submarine D-1*, 1935.

U.S. Government. "U.S. Warship—statistics and diagrams," 1960.

INDEX